Dear Readers,

Thank you for your letters. It is a great blessing for me to know that you are being helped by what I went through.

You are always with me, dear readers, and I hope my efforts to promote safe and healthy flying will benefit you, your colleagues, and your loved ones.

I often think about your letters, and have written all the chapters in **The Jet Safe & Easy Series** entirely in response to your comments and questions.

I write. . . I urge. . . I watch. . . I wait for change.

Stay well,
Diana Fairechild

—Andrew Weil, M.D.

"Diana Fairechild discusses all the health hazards endemic to modern air travel, and she suggests steps you can take to protect yourself."

—Uri Geller, spoon bender, author

"Diana Fairechild is a natural born healer. She was put on Earth to help millions of people. I really truly feel that Diana's motivation is to educate us, the people who fly—who could die on airplanes. Diana writes air travel books so people can learn how to protect themselves."

—The Direct Issue

"Fairechild's writing is the result of her own experience with flight-induced maladies. This book is actually a blessing in disguise as she has had to suffer a long recovery in order to offer sound advice to her readers."

—Noel Brown, M.D.
United Nations Environment Director

"I would like to distribute Jet Smart to my frequent flying colleagues."

—Environ

"Jet Smart dropped a bomb in Washington, and the Environmental Protection Agency and Department of Transportation changed policy."

—Meeting News
"Diana Fairechild tells you how to minimize the emotionally-draining and even the life-threatening effects of flying."

—Trade Winds
"Diana Fairechild lays claim to the distinction of being the first airline employee to blow the whistle on the airline industry for health hazards to which it has routinely subjected passengers and crew."

—Coleman Andrews, LA Times
"Fairechild spices up her book with no-nonsense insider's asides that are often simply fascinating.

—Howard Pierce, frequent flyer
"That which you have already accomplished is a great humanitarian concern. What could possibly be more important than for each of us to have air that is capable of sustaining a healthy life-style? Your fight has been a long one, and you have been doing it single-handedly to a large degree, but you have managed to catch the attention of a lot of people."

—Byron Dale, frequent flyer
"After flying on 64 airlines to 40 countries, I was burned out. Chronic jetlag, as you so appropriately explain it, should be the genesis of a sorely needed medical treatment."

Strategies for the Wise Passenger

Turbulence

Terrorism

Streaking

Cardiac Arrest

Too Tall

By

Diana Fairechild

Strategies for the Wise Passenger
Turbulence • Terrorism • Streaking
Cardiac Arrest • Too Tall

Library of Congress: 2003090332
1. air travel—safety & health 2. flight attendant

ISBN: 1-892997-73-8

Manufactured in the United States of America

Published By

flyana.com

PO Box 248 • Anahola, Hawaii 96703 • USA
808/ 828-1919

Table of Contents
Strategies for the Wise Passenger

Turbulence   19
How to avoid injuries during severe turbulence.

Terrorism   35
How you can recognize and defeat a terrorist.

Streaking   61
Flying naked and some aviation factoids.

Cardiac Arrest & Medical Emergencies   67
Surviving in-flight medical emergencies and
helping other passengers, too.

Too Tall   81
14 ways to beat the system when you are
over 6-feet tall.

—Art Bell, Coast to Coast AM

"I'm sick of getting sick on airplanes. I took a 757 down to Mazatlan, and I took a 757 back. And several days later, I got sick. Really sick. Now I went to China, and I got sick. And I went to Paris, and I got sick. I am sick of getting sick on airplanes. Hacking. Coughing. Sneezing. Yesterday, I was so out of it that when I was trying to fix something, I got super glue all over my hands. Then, like an idiot, I tried to pull the glue off with my teeth. I put a finger in my mouth, figuring it was already dry, and glued my lip shut. And that's how sick I was. I completely screwed up there. You might be able to tell, I'm a little bit angry. So I have contacted somebody who knows about airplanes. I want the real scoop. Her name is Diana Fairechild. We're going to ask her why you get sick on airplanes and how you can prevent it."

Acknowledgments

The Jet Safe & Easy Series has been in process since Jet Smart was published in 1992. Including the 14 years it initially took me to write Jet Smart, my published work in aviation safety and health has taken me 25 years of diligent research and writing to date.

If I had known at the start the commitment that would be required of me, I'm not sure I would have dared to begin. As it is, I have persevered both for my readers and for my own healing.

While writing and publishing the first book, Jet Smart, I was virtually working in a vacuum. Since then, thousands of readers have contacted me with their questions, and with financial support, too. Special thanks to R. William Andrew and Dr. Chris Breitenback, who both offered me grants for editing. This sequel to Jet Smart had become unwieldy with 70 chapters, and the grants gave it the benefit of a series of excellent editors.

I am very grateful to have worked with the following editors: Sara Held, Sylvia Partridge, Dave Sanford, Dove White, Nina Anderson, Kimberly Whitaker, Solarae, and Nan Williams. Thank you all for your heart-felt comments.

I sometimes run things by my friends and think of them as my personal board of directors. Thank you Peter Sanford, Linda Glas, Jim Gordon, George Ewing, M.D., Linda A. Evans, Joseph Ryan, Gerald Sterns, Dan Poynter, and Roger Silber.

Less frequent contacts, but no less important, took place with Jessica Brown, Jonathan Cender, Yvonne Conner, M.D., Siyanda Elizabeth, Eddy Free, Sandy Giminez, Patricia and Joseph Hanwright, Steven Krolick, Robin Mair, Mike Meador, Helaine Perel, Sandy Smith, Chris Thompson, Doug Walkinsaw, Haviland Wright, and the Hawaii state reseach librarians. Thank you.

Deep appreciation to Kauai photographer Winston Kawamoto for taking my photo for the cover and to Adam Prall who helped me with the cover elements.

I know I have left out people who have contributed to this Series. My airline insider contacts are a secret, of course, so they are not mentioned here. I thank all the mechanics, flight attendants, and pilots who regularly keep in touch.

My heartfelt thanks goes out to all my readers who came forward to assist me—and, especially for this volume, the tall people who wrote to me over the last seven years with their personal strategies for flying. I apologize for not being able to mention your names here. I had to change computers, from PC to Mac, and have not been able to recreate the archive. If you see your tip in this book, please contact me again.

I am truly very grateful for the interest and assistance of everyone who helped me to get this project off the ground. Thank you.

About this Series

The Jet Safe & Easy Series
Making the Skies Friendly Again

Each book in **The Jet Safe & Easy Series** is designed to inform and empower airline passengers and crew—even in situations where it may appear as if everything seems totally beyond one's control.

Some of the books in this 10-book series are arranged topically to be helpful to specific readers—such as pregnant passengers, frequent flyers, or even "freaking" flyers.

Other books include a variety of chapters of interest to all passengers seeking safer, healthier, and more comfortable flying.

The author of the Series, Diana Fairechild, is an airline stewardess turned airline reform advocate. The body of work that Fairechild has amassed over the last decade springs from her unswerving devotion to improve conditions for air travelers.

The Series is based on Fairechild's 21 years as an international flight attendant; her interviews with scientists, aviation specialists, and physicians; and the questions and experiences of thousands of airline passengers who continue to write to her.

Fairechild began her work as an air safety advocate by writing, publishing, and publicizing the ground-breaking book **Jet Smart** in 1992, which became a best seller with in excess of 50,000 copies sold.

In **Jet Smart**, Fairechild was the first to expose the harmful practice of "disinsection" (spraying pesticide ON passengers while trying to kill insects). **Jet Smart** also revealed to an unsuspecting public the dangers of toxic cabin air and water, and why sudden illnesses "mysteriously" occur after flying.

Today, Fairechild's writing has become a vital part of the fabric that makes up the public's view of flying—so much so that her words often flow anonymously from many who write, report, and speak about air travel safety and health.

As time passes, Fairechild's warnings about airline cabin health and safety hazards have been validated. For example, it is now public knowledge that pesticides sprayed on flights can be deadly; that frequent flying diminishes brain function; and that cramped seating along with low air pressure contributes to deep vein thrombosis.

Fairechild's writing takes us on an exciting journey packed with critical information and useful safety tips on the realities of air travel. Though we may embark feeling uneasy, by the time we land at the end of each chapter, we feel reassured because we know what we need to do to take care of ourselves—and we've had a few laughs along the way.

At this point in her career, Fairechild has either written for, appeared on, or been quoted by nearly every major media source, including ABC,

NBC, CNN, *Forbes*, *USA Today*, *TIME*, *The New York Times*, *Business Week*, *The Wall Street Journal*, and the *International Herald Tribune*.

In addition to her pioneering work in air travel, Fairechild has authored two books on other subjects. *NONI: Aspirin of the Ancients* offers readers information on how Fairechild used a Hawaiian herb to detoxify after flying 10 million miles and working for two decades in the toxic airplane environment. *Office Yoga: At-Your-Desk Exercises* was inspired by the thousands of hours she has now spent as a writer at a computer; it was featured on the front page of *The Wall Street Journal* in 2002.

Today, Fairechild is in demand as a speaker; at the podium, she occasionally lapses into performing a life jacket demonstration for her audiences.

She also serves as an expert witness in law cases of flight-related death and injury; is founder of The Fair Air Coalition, a nonprofit advocacy group for passengers; and is web master of flyana.com, her extensive web site—"One of the 12 Most Creative Web Sites" according to *The New York Times*.

In response to a CNN-TV producer who contacted her in 2002 about a travel show they wanted to do on gadgets for frequent flyers, Fairechild replied: "The traveler's best gadget is himself. And the best way to use this gadget is to have the most information available. Providing good solid information is what I do."

—John Bogert,
Copley Newspapers

"The thing I enjoy only slightly less than a tooth extraction is flying, especially long flights to London—which, by the way, Fairechild calls one of the worst journeys imaginable because it goes west to east (the worst direction for jet lag), exposes the body to higher degrees of radiation on its polar route, and can, magically, make 12 hours in a teeny seat feel like three years in a Roman galley. When you think about it, that's a pretty amazing collection of discomforts for a service touted in the ads as a colorful adventure. Fairechild, still perky after what amounts to 300 circumnavigations of the globe, said that the mostly non-lethal dangers of air travel amount to one of the great unexplored environmental health issues of the day. There's a lot of talk in this quite incredible book about cost cutting showing up in unchanged air filters and dirty blankets. Considering how many of us this affects, this lone voice is well worth hearing."

Dedication

To flight attendants worldwide—
Also known as stewardess,
Stew, steward, stewardii,
Purser, chief purser,
Air hostess, sky girl,
Hey miss, you-hoo,
Cabin attendant
And cabin crew.

Turbulence Strategy ★1. **Standing?**

If you are walking or standing in the aisle when "severe turbulence" hits, sit down on the floor and hold on to the railing below any seat.

Turbulence Strategy ★2. **In Your Seat?**

Any time turbulence hits, buckle up.

Turbulence Strategy ★3. **Lavatory?**

During turbulence, close the bowl lid (so the blue stuff doesn't splash on you) and hold on to the handrail.

Turbulence Strategy ★4. **Laptop?**

During "severe turbulence" shut your laptop—not just "sleep mode." A big bump could still jar it on. With a spinning hard drive and another bounce, your drive could crash. Stash your laptop on the floor in front of you with your toes preventing it from sliding or bouncing.

Turbulence Strategy ★5. **Eating?**

If your food is popping off your tray, cover it with a blanket or newspaper and stash the tray under the seat in front of you.

Turbulence

"What is really happening on the plane when they say, 'We've entered turbulence. Make sure that your seatbelts are on'? If I knew what happens to the plane when turbulence hits, I might not be so frightened."

This chapter offers a full explanation about what happens on board before and after you hear the announcement, "Ladies and gentlemen, please fasten your seatbelts."

You will learn what causes turbulence, what are the different types of turbulence, why pilots can't always predict it, and what pilots do to keep the plane safe during turbulence.

You will also find suggestions on how you can prevent turbulence-related injuries. Contrary to industry rhetoric, the seatbelt rule is not the only answer.

"Fasten Your Seatbelts"

"There is a famous turbulence reference from Hollywood in the 1950 film, "All About Eve." Bette Davis, playing a Hollywood diva, says this line with a sultry smile on her lips and diamonds glittering at her ears.

The diva, poised on a staircase looking down into a room full of friends, says, "Fasten your seatbelts; it's going to be a bumpy night."

In the 50 years since Bette Davis said "Fasten your seatbelts; it's going to be a bumpy night," she has been quoted a million times—by stock brokers, insurance brokers, politicians, and judges —whenever someone wanted to imply: Watch out for me now! Trouble is my middle name.

More Hollywood Turbulence

In the 1980 film, "Airplane," turbulence hits while a passenger is putting on lipstick, and the red lipstick streaks from the corner of her mouth across her cheek to the top of her ear.

In a later scene, the same lady is applying green eye shadow during turbulence. This time her finger slides off her eyelid and trails a bright green line down the bridge of her nose.

The 1998 film, "Blackout Effect," is not a comedy. During turbulence, the captain comes on the PA and says, "Ladies and gentleman, we are experiencing moderate turbulence." Then a tray falls out of a meal cart, a flight attendant gets thrown down to the floor, and the pilots request air traffic control for a change of altitude.

If you want to see horrific air turbulence scenes, watch the 1999 film, "Freefall." Un-belted actors are thrown around the cabin. Then the overhead bins pop open, and luggage rains down on everyone. One piece of luggage hits an FAA inspector on the head.

Turbulence Strategy ★6. **Click It**

Make sure the overhead bin isn't packed so tightly that it could pop open. When you slam it shut, listen for the latch to "click" shut and test that it is, in fact, firmly shut.

Turbulence Strategy ★7. **Rearranging**

Passengers seated on the aisles have my permission to rearrange the contents of any overhead bins that are nearby.

Turbulence Strategy ★8. **Heavy Bags**

Heavy bags are safer stowed under the seat in front of you, or checked in—or better yet, shipped ahead.

It's true—passengers sometimes get injured during turbulence, and occasionally, even mortally wounded by luggage falling from overhead bins.[1]

From a reader (12/99): "While working as a well-paid translator accompanying a Japanese CEO, a bag fell on my head during turbulence, knocking me unconscious. After suffering disorientation, memory loss, and severe depression, my work as a traveling translator is no longer possible. The airline refused any compensation, refused to give me the name of the owner of the bag, and most importantly, did not offer an apology."

Turbulence Strategy ★9. **Night Flight**

On night flights, fasten your seatbelt outside your blanket. If there is turbulence while you sleep, stews will see that your seatbelt is fastened and leave you in peace.

Turbulence Strategy ★10. **Not Tight**

Airlines request us to wear seatbelts "low and tight," but I prefer a slack seatbelt. Even though a seatbelt isn't tugging at my gut, it still keeps me in my seat whenever there is turbulence, but it allows me to squirm, which is so much easier on my back.

What Causes Turbulence?

Turbulence is caused by changes in the air that airplanes fly through. Air is not a uniform. Just like the sea, the air has currents, as well as random wakes and bumps from other planes, heat coming up from the ground, sinking air over cold bodies of water, and on and on.

Pilots refer to different types of turbulence. For example, "convective turbulence" is caused by thunderstorms, and "mechanical turbulence" is caused by the wake of another airplane. "Clear-air turbulence" occurs when there are changes in the temperature and wind.

The Jet Stream Is Wind

Planes crisscross the world every day in jet streams because this helps them fly faster.

The jet stream that I am most familiar with is the polar jet stream, in which I flew over 300 round-trips to Europe from the West Coast of the U.S. With the wind at your back flying east, the flight time to Europe is invariably several hours shorter than the westbound flight from Europe.

An old airline sign-off among pilots is, "May the wind always be at your back." When you catch a jet stream, the wind is at your back, and it reduces your flight time and your fuel consumption.

However, when there is a change from low-speed to high-speed wind as aircraft move into jet streams, clear-air turbulence often occurs.[2]

Pilots Try

Pilots can't always predict turbulence, though they try to warn each other of turbulent skies by radio from one plane to the next.

Your pilot will also get weather updates from air traffic control along the route.

Pilots actually take off with only a flight plan and a general knowledge of what to expect. Then they "feel their way" into the weather, continually correcting the original flight plan for previously unknown factors such as wind, rain, air pockets, and currents.

If something doesn't feel right, the pilots ask air traffic control for permission to change the altitude or the latitude (the distance to the polar caps).

Meanwhile, pilots continuously perform a series of changes, reassessing the aircraft's flight plan; they "fly on a heading," check it and adjust, fly some more, check it and adjust. No pilot expects a flight to progress without adapting to the many variables which arise and were not planned beforehand on the ground.

On airline route maps, it appears as if airplanes fly in a straight line from one airport to the next. But in actuality, planes always go off course, and then they have to be brought back on course either mechanically by autopilot or manually by the pilot. Pilots are trained to get the plane back on course.

When turbulence hits, this is just another adjustment that the pilots (or autopilot) have to make.

Injuries

In rare instances, a pilot may not handle the aircraft properly during turbulence—for example, on night flights when he may not be as alert.

In a precedent-setting case, a Japan Airlines captain was indicted (5/02) for professional negligence when turbulence hit.

The captain failed to switch off the autopilot before taking manual control, resulting in severe injuries to 6 passengers and 8 stews. One stew died after 20 months in a hospital.[3]

Another example of severe turbulence hit between Ft. Lauderdale and Pittsburgh on USAir.[4] All stews plus one infant hit the ceiling repeatedly. The baby was okay; the stews had broken limbs and broken teeth. A number of passengers were injured when glass from broken liquor bottles and ceiling lights, as well as lasagna-laden meal trays, rained down on them.

Flight Attendants Fly Around

Hard hats should really be a part of the stew uniform. It's not a bad idea for passengers, either.

Most turbulence injuries are suffered by stews. When I was flying, stews were not permitted to sit down during turbulence unless the captain came on the PA and told us to sit. I didn't wait for the announcement. I felt that I should be the primary judge of when it was unsafe for me to be standing during turbulence, so I sat down whenever turbulence was too rough or made me too queasy.

In truth, pilots may not know how rough it is in the cabin since turbulence is generally mildest in the cockpit and most severe in the aft. Today, some airlines now permit stews to use their own judgment during turbulence.

Turbulence Strategy ★11. **Crew Care**
When there is "severe turbulence" on board, if you see a flight attendant in the aisle, offer her a steady hand—even a lap.

Save A Stew

A friend of mine said she "levitated" once in severe turbulence, and she doesn't even remember landing—she's a wind surfer, so sea legs are normal for her. Another friend had the beverage cart land on her during turbulence, breaking her leg.

A big problem for stews is that when turbulence hits, their crew seats may not be close enough to reach, or they may not be available. Crew seats are often used during meal services to hold cartons of soft drinks or are piled up with used trays.

What's infinitely worse for stews is that during turbulence, the crew seats can actually be quite hazardous. I used to get a twinge of fear on every takeoff and landing when I was facing heavy carts that were prevented from crushing me only by the integrity of little latches.

One day during turbulence, while sitting on my crew seat, a coffeepot from the galley came flying at me. I ducked just in time.

In severe turbulence, the safest place for a stew may be sitting in any available passenger seat near where she is working, or even on the floor.

If I were crouching in the aisle, I would certainly appreciate a passenger reaching out to help hold me down.

During severe turbulence, if you see a blue blur as a flight attendant flies through the air, try to catch her. You might save her life.

As for the coffeepots and trays, the safest thing to do during turbulence is to throw a blanket over them and then put your feet on top.

What To Do

A reader wrote to *Aviation Week* (5/28/98), "A system that aerodynamically loads an aircraft in the opposite direction of a gust would eliminate the hazard of turbulence."[5] Translation: If turbulence is pushing a plane in a certain direction and the pilot can counteract that force enough, then inside the cabin there will be no bumpiness.

For the most part, the aircraft's automatic pilot is responsive in this way, but it does this generally, rather than to every subtle jolt, and it also may not respond as fast as we would like it to.

If more resources were earmarked for the problem of turbulence, I believe this problem would quickly be resolved. It would be wonderful if something could be done to prevent turbulence-related injuries—there are too many incidents and too many injuries.

Chronology Of Turbulence

• In 1997, a flight from Tokyo to Honolulu plunged in severe turbulence, killing one woman and injuring 83 people.[6]

• In 1998, after a flight between Seattle and Las Vegas, six people were treated at a hospital for neck and back injuries, and one flight attendant had a broken ankle.

• In 1999, on a flight to Hong Kong, 47 people suffered head and neck injuries, one with a fractured spine.[8]

• In 2000, Honolulu paramedics met a flight from Tokyo and treated five flight attendants and three passengers, including an 18-month-old infant.[9]

• In 2001, a plane crashed just outside New York's JFK Airport, killing everyone on board. Seconds before the crash, severe turbulence caused the aircraft's vertical fin to break off.[10]

• In 2002, a flight from Sydney diverted to Auckland after severe turbulence left flight attendants with broken legs and back injuries, and three passengers were hospitalized later as well.[11]

• In 2003, a flight from Maui landed in San Francisco after severe turbulence. Several flight attendants, as they were clearing meals, had been bounced against the cabin ceiling. San Francisco paramedics treated ten people, seven of whom were injured badly enough to be hospitalized.[12]

Turbulence Strategy ★12. **Prayer**

Dear God, please assist the pilots in having the ability to get this plane back into smooth air and give this flight a happy landing.

Buckle Up Is Not Enough

There is a proposed FAA seatbelt rule that would require passengers to keep their seatbelts fastened all throughout their flights.

I am not in favor of this rule. We need to walk around and exercise in order to help prevent deep vein thrombosis and other health problems related to sitting without moving for long periods in the low air pressure environment on the plane.

And what about stews? For the passengers' sake, when severe turbulence hits, stews get busy securing the cabin, instead of sitting down and buckling up as they would like.

Flight attendants always make an effort to put on a calm face for passengers. When stews were first hired in the 30s, their original responsibility—which still continues today—was to put on a brave face. The first thing passengers do when there is turbulence is to look at the faces of flight attendants. The airlines really need to address the problem of their cabin crews regularly being injured during turbulence.

Turbulence Strategy ★13. **For Government**
Telling people to keep their seatbelts fastened is a band-aid approach to turbulence. It's time to use technology to handle turbulence.

Use Technology

It's time to use technology to avoid injuries from turbulence. *A Wall Street Journal* writer said it perfectly, "It's time to step up efforts to harness more high-tech measures to forecast and spot the atmospheric conditions that can toss about a jet in mid air."[13] That was in 1997, but still nothing has been done!

"We can do much to steer clear of turbulence," reads an editorial in *Aviation Week*, "but it will take an effort that goes far beyond just pleading for passengers to buckle up."[14]

Dare Devils

From a reader (10/02): "How is it that a plane can hit unexpected turbulence that causes it to suddenly drop over 5,000 feet? I like roller coasters, but in a plane, a drop like that is scary. Is there any way to predict this?"

Answer: When an airplane, flying 500 mph, flies into a column of high-speed downward moving air, the airplane naturally gets pushed down.

The plane will regain its original altitude only after it has passed through the column of air. While a plane is dropping, the sudden loss of altitude increases air speed. The pilots then use this increased air speed to help the plane pull up. For pilots, it's perfectly routine.

No doubt, pilots feel easier up front than we do in the back of the plane—just as the driver of a car can be blasé about twists and turns that may disturb those of us in the back seat.

It is a rare individual who can find fun in turbulence on airplanes. I have met only a few, one a recent tourist in Hawaii. His wife was complaining about the turbulence on the flight over. He smiled quietly and said it was fun. It reminded him of a "carnival ride."

For certain types of people—surfers and bungee jumpers, for example—adjusting to the changing elements of nature gives them a high. But for most of us, when the elements take control of a plane, it makes us wonder if we're going to die.

When Pigs Fly

In December 2000, a 300-pound pig flew in the first row of first class without a seatbelt on a 6-hour flight between Philadelphia and Seattle.

When the owner of the pig made her reservation, she asked to bring along with her a 13-pound "therapeutic companion pet."

She then showed up with a 300-pound pig, claiming she was unable to cope on a flight without the company of her pet pig.

She was also unable to control the pig, it later turned out.[15]

This was a Vietnamese potbelly pig, more often referred to as something for dinner in Vietnam, and certainly not something that would fly in first class without a seatbelt.

On the flight, the pig was reported to have become "unruly"—an airline term previously reserved only for human passengers.

The unruly pig ran up the aisle squealing, and even bashed the cockpit door. Flight attendants were eventually able to stop this unruly behavior by throwing food at the pig—specifically, banana-nut muffins.

If you showed up with 300 pounds of extra luggage, the airlines would most certainly charge you $375 in excess fees, but for some reason, this unruly potbelly pig got to fly for free.

For me, "When Pigs Fly" proves that there is no FAA regulation without an exception. Here, the FAA concluded that U.S. Airways had acted properly when it permitted a 300-pound pig to fly in the first row of first class without a seatbelt.

Geez. I think about all the times that I—along with thousands of other stews—have told passengers: "Buckle up, it's an FAA regulation." Ð

> ## Turbulence Strategy ★14. **Activism**
> Passengers and crew need to demand that the airlines and their partners in government effectively address turbulence.

References
[1] PA News, "The terror of turbulence," 4/14/99.

[2] Airwise News, "JAL captain faces death allegations," 5/20/02.

[3] Reuters (Pittsburgh), "Flight 333," 8/30/88.

[4] UPI (Tenn.), "Severe hailstorm," 5/8/98.

[5] *Aviation Week*, "Correspondence," 5/25/98.

[6] *The Wall Street Journal*, "Turbulence resists an easy fix," 12/30/97.

[7] Reuters (Seattle), "Turbulence," 3/4/98.

[8] AP (Hong Kong), "47 Injured," 10/4/99.

[9] AP (Honolulu), "Passengers Injured," 1/10/00.

[10] www.newsmax.com, "Flight 587: Should we suspect terrorism," 1/14/02.

[11] AP (New Zealand), "United jet hits severe turbulence," 5/5/02.

[12] *Los Angeles Times*, "10 hurt as plane to S.F. plunges" 3/14/03.

[13] *The Wall Street Journal*, "Turbulence," 12/30/97

[14] *Aviation Week*, "Viewpoint," 1/19/98.

[15] www.thelocalplanet.com, "When Pigs Fly," 12/14/00.

33

Terrorism Strategy ★1. **Confidence**

As long as we are living and active, there will be something we can do to help obstruct terrorists. We know that terrorists can be overcome by a group of passengers, and when passengers are joined together, they are stronger than any terrorists, no matter what weapons the terrorists may be brandishing.

Terrorism Strategy ★2. **Cell phones**

It is known that passengers on the 9-11 hijacked planes placed calls from their cell phones. Cell phones only work when planes are flying below 10,000 feet (approximately). On 9-11, all the hijacked planes were flying low. Normally, cell phones only work during the takeoff and landing phases of flight.

Terrorism

September 11, 2001: Terrorists hijack 4 planes over the East Coast of the United States. This event will forever be known as 9-11, the same numbers we dial for help in an emergency.

American Airlines Flight #11

Flight #11, headed for the West Coast loaded with fuel, wings away from Boston at about 8 a.m.

Flight Crew. After terrorists penetrate the cockpit, the captain secretly keys his microphone so air traffic control can hear everything that is said in the cockpit. "We have more planes," they hear.

Cabin Crew. After terrorists take control of the cabin, an off-duty flight attendant manages to telephone the airport. She tells a supervisor that two stews have been stabbed by terrorists, whom she identifies by their seat numbers—thus providing investigators with crucial information.

About 45 minutes after takeoff, flight #11 crashes into the 110-story north tower of the World Trade Center. For the next 18 minutes, the media speculates about a possible aircraft mechanical failure.

During these 18 minutes, even President Bush, according to *The Washington Post*, thought that the World Trade Center tragedy was actually "an accident involving a small twin-engine plane."[1]

United Airlines Flight #175

United flight #175 is another early morning departure from Boston, also to the West Coast. After the terrorists take over #175, the plane heads, instead, straight for Manhattan, flying at 500 miles per hour—more than double the legal air-speed limit over the Hudson Valley.

At 9:03 a.m., #175 crashes into the World Trade Center, striking the south tower in an almost vertical position—with its wings full with fuel— hitting as many floors of the WTC as possible.

American Airlines Flight #77

Using cell phones, a number of passengers on flight #77 report the hijacking in progress.

At 9:40 a.m., flight #77 crashes into the Pentagon, damaging one side of our five-sided U.S. military command center.

Twin Towers Collapse

At 10:05 a.m., the south tower of the World Trade Center collapses. About a half hour later, the north tower collapses, with the eyes of a global audience glued to their TVs.

Heroes On United Flight #93

After terrorists take over flight #93, passengers learn of the other 3 hijackings from cell phone calls to colleagues and families.

Seeing the bigger picture, a few passengers decide to make an effort to protect those of us on the ground,[2] and they succeed! Diverting the plane from another "significant target," flight #93 crashes in rural Pennsylvania.[3]

In their effort to divert flight #93 from a "significant target," at least 5 passengers braved the terrorists to get to the cockpit—about 100 feet from the back of the 757.

One of these passengers was a weightlifter, another a judo champion. One was the son of a flight attendant. The wife of another later told the press that her husband's courage was a blessing that would help her family through the years ahead.

Indeed. This blessing has already helped many of us. In the midst of so much tragedy, the heroes of flight #93 help us to hope—we know now that passengers *can* overcome terrorists.

Land Immediately

After the twin towers collapse, the airways over the Continental U.S. are closed. "Land ASAP at the nearest airport," orders air traffic control.

From a Flight Attendant (9/11/01): "As the North Atlantic airways were vacated, Gander [East Coast, Canada] ended up with 53 planes from all over the world.

"The population of Gander is 10,400. The population from the 53 planes was 10,500.

Terrorism Strategy ★3. **Empathy**

Friendliness cuts down on stress for everyone, and it can also be comforting to assess others in a non-emergency mode, noting those we may want to count on. In addition, I suggest that when we fly we make it a practice to look out for elderly travelers, or others who may need a helping hand or a smiling face—travel is more difficult now for them, too.

"All the high schools around Gander were used to lodge the 'plane people.' The elderly, however, were accommodated in private homes. Everyone was offered food, showers, laundry facilities, free boat cruises of the lakes, and guided hikes in the forests.

"Two days later, when the airways opened, on at least one flight leaving Gander, the 'plane people' passed the hat. In a few minutes, $29,000 was collected to start a college scholarship fund for the children of Lewisporte—the village where they had received a most gracious hospitality."

Changing Attitudes

3,047 people died as a result of the 9-11 terrorist acts. 3,251 children lost a parent.[5] 25 flight attendants died on the 4 hijacked planes.

38

We mourn for all these souls, and we mourn the loss of our pervasive sense of security.

Until 9-11, as Americans, we took our security for granted.

Marilyn Monroe poignantly reflects this ingrained American sense of security in her 1957 film, "The Prince and the Showgirl." Monroe's character overhears a conspirator's plot, and when threatened, she says, "I'm an American citizen. Nobody can do anything to me."

After 9-11, Americans realized they no longer had the luxury of taking their homeland security for granted.

The New Reality

Our new national insecurity has opened the door to a different way of life.

Since 9-11, airports reflect a new sense of sobriety. It's not just the military guards with rifles. Passengers are now more patient with the airlines and more restrained as their possessions are shuffled through and rearranged.

Passengers appear simply grateful to be able to pick up the pieces of their business and family life that require travel.

After the physical and mental devastation of 9-11 was sifted through and carted away, the aviation industry sifts through its work force and struggles with declining business.

The Big Questions

Since 9-11, many questions about security are being asked and slowly answered. What needs to be done to create really effective security? Does increased security make flying difficult in other ways? more costly? impossibly inconvenient? What should passengers do if their plane is hijacked? Should you travel with a cell phone? Should you avoid certain destinations? airlines? flying times?

Speaking personally, I continue to fly and feel that risk taking is a necessary aspect of living, a part of the process of exploring our world.

In our present atmosphere of uncertainty, questions about security are not likely to disappear soon. But I have done my utmost to offer you my thoughts and strategies in this chapter, and also in future volumes in the **Jet Safe & Easy Series**, which specifically address security issues at airports and on airplanes. Also, please check my web site for continuing updates.

Terrorism Strategy ★4. **Be Brave**

Since it's not possible to know for sure what the future holds, let's live bravely, so that when all is said and done, we've really lived, instead of cowered in reaction to speculations of the future that might not happen.

Terrorism Strategy ★5. **Be Calm**
Reduce stress in your daily life. Just say "no" to stress when it rears its ugly head. If you practice peacefulness, then in a stressful environment such as an airplane cabin, you will be better able to function from a place of calm. This will leave more options open should anything untoward arise.

Hijacking Goes Back a Long Way

Prior to 9-11, airline pilots were instructed to cooperate with hijackers. The philosophy was that if the hijackers did not damage the plane, then we would take them wherever they wanted.

In the 1972 film, "Skyjacked," when the captain (played by Charlton Heston) finds out from a note that his plane has a terrorist aboard, he holds a briefing for the stews. He tells them, "Keep it normal. Keep it light. Keep your heads."

At that time, in my real-life stew training, our instructor actually told us (I swear!), "Hijackers are afraid of women, so you don't need to let them in the cockpit. Block the door."

Glamorous Hijacking To Italy

In 1969, Raphael Minichiello hijacked a plane between Los Angeles and San Francisco.

Raphael (Raff) then forced, at gunpoint, a series of pilots to fly him to Italy—via Denver (where passengers got off), to New York (new pilots came on board), to Maine (the plane was refueled), across the Atlantic to Ireland, and finally to Rome.[6]

In Italy, Raff was eventually caught at the Sanctuary of the Madonna of Divine Love.

Raff had been a decorated U.S. Vietnam vet facing a court marshal for a PX burglary when he hijacked the plane in California.

After a brief jail term in Rome, Raff became a national hero in Italy, with marriage proposals from Italian women and, according to rumors, a movie contract from Carlo Ponti, Sophia Loren's producer husband.

Glamorous Hijacking With Parachute

In 1971, after a normal takeoff from Portland (Oregon), D. B. Cooper handed a note to the crew that said, "I have a bomb in my brief case."

Cooper then demanded $200,000 in $20 bills, plus 4 parachutes, and to be flown to Mexico City. After he got his demands at a transit stop, Cooper parachuted out from the 727's back stairs, which drop from the tail of the plane. (All 727's were subsequently retrofitted so that the aft stairs could not be opened in flight.)

Cooper was never seen again, but he has become a folk hero. Check it out on the Internet.

There are dozens of web pages honoring D.B. Cooper, a song about D.B. Cooper, and even recurring D.B. Cooper look-a-like contests.

At the time of the hijacking, the aircraft belonged to Northwest Airlines. The plane was later sold to Key Airlines, a now defunct charter company based in Georgia.

On all their charter flights, the plane's infamy was publicized—until they discovered that passengers were so enthralled with the glamorous hijacking that they were taking the plane apart.

Exit signs, armrests, everything removable, disappeared as souvenirs of the famous hijacking.

Take Me To Cuba

Between 1968 and 1985, there were 182 successful hijackings to Cuba—113 initiated from inside the continental U.S.[7]

Hijackers to Cuba always demanded money from passengers. In those days, there was a story circulating among crews that passengers leaving Miami had become so blasé during hijackings that they actually gave money to the hijackers without even looking up from their newspapers.

Since there was no official service by U.S. carriers to Cuba at that time, and since our pilots were instructed to take these hijackers wherever they wanted, Pan Am secretly issued all pilots leaving Miami route maps to Havana.

Hijacking Becomes Terrorism

The 1985 hijacking of a TWA jet marks the commencement of aviation terrorism. This TWA hijacking in Athens was an organized act of terrorism with many strange twists.

At a refueling stop in Algiers, the hijackers insisted on Shell fuel—because they believed that Shell was an Arab-owned company.

Next, the U.S. embassy refused to pay for the gas, and the airport would not start pumping without a Shell credit card.

The chief purser then charged 6,000 gallons at $1 a gallon on her own credit card.

Tragically, at Beirut Airport an American passenger was shot, then tossed out of the opened front door of the plane onto the tarmac.

Immediately afterwards, the Hezbollah Shi-ite Muslim terrorist who shot the American told the chief purser that American bombings of Beirut had killed his wife and baby girl.

This terrorist then asked the chief purser to sing a song to him—and she did.

Captain Testrake, in his 1987 book about the hijacking, actually bragged that he continuously lied to the terrorists, telling them, for example, that the aircraft had engine trouble so it couldn't take off from Beirut.

He said that the terrorists, not being pilots, couldn't dispute what he told them.

Wealthy passengers offered the hijackers $3 million in cash to release them. Most of the passengers were then released, but 39 passengers were kept as hostages at several locations around the city of Beirut for 17 days!

The pilots, however, were kept as hostages on the airplane, also for 17 days, while other planes took off and landed on the same tarmac.

Occasionally, a cleaning lady even came on board. And several sets of captors came and went, stealing the plane's blankets, pillows, O_2 and CO_2 bottles, escape slides, and everything of value from the passengers' and crew luggage.

The terrorists released all the hostages on the 17th day, exchanging them for 766 Shiite Muslim prisoners held by the Israelis.

After this, our crew layovers were changed over to Teheran because our Pan Am around-the-world service skipped Beirut. And on all our flights through the Middle East, we carried air marshals.

Today, when I think about Beirut, it's not terrorism that snags my mind, but the dozens of Beirut layovers that I was privileged to have there.

At the Phoenicia Intercontinental Hotel, our crews were offered awesome hospitality. Each time we stews entered the lobby, we were greeted with tiny cups of aromatic Turkish coffee on a brass serving tray accompanied by a chorus of "Welcome home" from the bellboys.

Terrorism Strategy ★6. **For the FAA**

All information regarding terrorist threats must be made public. Passengers have the right to know and make their own decisions.

Pan Am Bombing Over Lockerbie

In 1988, Pan Am's flight #103 blew up over Lockerbie, Scotland, killing everyone on board—259 people from 21 countries with ages ranging from 2 months to 82 years. Also killed were 11 residents of the little town of Lockerbie when debris from #103 rained down.

An alarming facet of the Pan Am #103 air disaster was something the press referred to as the "Helsinki warning." Several days before the bombing, the U.S. State Department had received a tip that a Pan Am flight to New York would be targeted by militant Muslims because two Jewish couriers would be on board carrying a huge delivery of diamonds from Amsterdam to New York.

Diplomats around the world had the luxury of not flying on #103—but the flying public was not warned.

After the bombing, Scotland Yard, the FBI and CIA, and the Scottish police searched through #103's debris scattered over 850 square miles, looking for evidence and the diamonds.

More than a decade after the bombing, the case was tried by 3 Scottish judges, and the former head of security for Libyan Arab Airlines was convicted and given a life sentence in Scotland.

By then, Pan Am had gone bankrupt, and David Thomson, a 10-year-old child in Lockerbie at the time of the Pan Am disaster, was enrolled at Syracuse University (New York) on a scholarship.

The scholarship was set up by families of the 35 Syracuse University students who lost their lives on Pan Am #103 after touring Europe.[8]

Passengers Participate

From a reader (9/02): "Should passengers participate in fighting terrorists when we fly?"

Answer: Yes, if you want to. Of course, you don't have to volunteer to do anything if you don't feel like it.

Participating in onboard security used to be exclusively the responsibility of the crew—but not anymore. Since 9-11, airline crews have been advised to rely on the support and information of passengers—and even direct passengers when they need help in maintaining onboard security.

Luckily, passengers have volunteered when needed, such as during the incident with the "shoe bomb terrorist"—when passengers helped stews to save the day, making it possible for that flight to have a happy landing.

How It Used To Be

The days when air travelers were expected to be passive about onboard security are long gone. In the 1996 film, "Panic in the Skies," you can see an example of how passengers used to be excluded from participating in onboard security.

In that film, after the cockpit was struck by lightning and all the pilots were dead, the stews gathered in a huddle, nervously trying to figure out how to land the plane, when a passenger walks up and says, "Can I help?"

Kate Jackson, in a perfect imitation of an authoritarian flight attendant, points her finger at this passenger and says, "Sit down. You are in violation of FAA regulations."

The passenger sat down, and after a number of subplots, Kate Jackson lands the plane!

Today, when there is an emergency, you won't find the Kate Jackson-type shaking her finger. If your stew needs help, she will yell, just like the stew on the plane with the shoe bomber.

The Shoe Bomb Terrorist

On December 22, 2001, Richard Reid, a recent convert to a militant sect of Islam, boarded American Airlines flight #63 in Paris on a suicide mission. At cruise altitude, he came within seconds of succeeding by almost detonating explosives concealed in his shoes.

Reid was seated near the center fuel tank. There is actually a terrorist precedent for detonating explosives near the center fuel tank on Philippine Airlines flight #434 (12/94).[9]

On #434, a bomb was placed under a seat in the life jacket pouch. As it turned out, the life jacket blunted the force of the explosion, so the fuel did not ignite, and the crippled plane landed safely.

Reid's shoes, however, were touching the floor, and he was in a window seat. The explosion Reid had been planning was to have pierced the fuselage and ignited the fuel.

It is obvious that the terrorists are learning from their mistakes. And passengers are learning, too!

Passengers Thwart Reid

On Reid's flight from Paris, a passenger named Arlette was sitting behind Reid. On first seeing Reid, Arlette told her husband, "He smells bad and he looks scary."[10]

A couple of hours later, Arlette was the first to smell the sulfur from the matches Reid was lighting, trying to ignite the explosives in his shoes. Arlette called a flight attendant, touched her finger to her nose, and pointed to Reid.

Reid's body was turned toward the window, so the flight attendant thought at first that he was smoking.

49

Then she saw that Reid was trying to light wires coming from his shoe! She grabbed Reid. He bit her. Then she yelled, "Heeeeeelp!"

Meanwhile, Arlette roused her husband from a nap. Then he and all the passengers in the vicinity did whatever they could to thwart Reid.

A dozen men wrestled Reid to the ground. They pulled their belts out of their trousers to tie him up. A physician injected Reid with a sedative. And one passenger stood guard with a fire extinguisher until after landing.

El Al Foils Reid

Five months earlier (7/01), Reid flew on El Al Airlines to Israel. El Al security profilers found him suspicious, so they conducted "rigorous checks of all the items he was carrying."[11]

Then, even after finding nothing specific, they assigned Reid a seat on the plane next to an armed air marshal. The extra searches on Reid and the guard on board are examples of how of how El Al security profilers acted on their intuition.

Access Intuition

An offensive odor or a frightening appearance on a passenger can be a clue that something is amiss. All air travelers will feel safer on board if they take the time to access their intuition both in the gate area and on board.

Terrorism Strategy ★7. **Intuition**

When you fly, turn up the rheostat on your intuition. Passengers who have practiced the skill of accessing their intuition will help everyone to feel safer on airplanes and really, truly be safer, too.

Terrorism Strategy ★8. **Gate Area**

Walk around the gate area for exercise, and while you're at it, make a note of other passengers you might want to call upon in an emergency. If you see someone who looks threatening, report it to your airline. If airline employees are too busy, call the airline's reservations number, the FBI: 202 324-3000, or call 911.

Accessing intuition is not new. When we meet people, there's always an instantaneous knowing about them. It's not only the way people look and smell, but also how we feel in their presence.

Using intuition, we can sense data from a super-normal, more subtle dimension and bring it forward into the practical world.

Passengers outnumber airline employees, and passengers have more time than employees to "tune in" to their fellow travelers.

Intuition – Two Examples

Intuition Example #1. James Woods' hunch. Actor James Woods (you may not know the name, but you would surely recognize his face)[12] was on a flight from Boston to Los Angeles just one month prior to the hijackings of 9-11.

As an actor, Woods is a trained observer, and intuitively, he had such a strong feeling on that flight that several of the passengers were terrorists that he asked a flight attendant to let him speak to the captain.[13] He did, but nothing was done about his hunch.

One month later, Woods was proved right. On 9-11, the records show that two of the men from Woods' flight were terrorists on the doomed planes.

Intuition Example #2. Cristina's bite marks. A second example for accessing intuition involves Cristina, the flight attendant who was bitten by Richard Reid.

Terrorism Strategy ★9. **Before Takeoff**

When you first board the aircraft, if you feel strongly that something on the plane is not right, tell the chief purser (usually at the front of the plane)—or even walk off the plane while it is still on the ground.

Terrorism Strategy ★10. **Alcohol**
When you fly, try to avoid drinking alcohol, because your chances of handling and surviving anything beyond what is normal, or what you may have anticipated, improve greatly if you are sober.

Cristina told the press what she thought when Reid didn't eat anything on that 10-hour flight from Paris: "Usually I'm happy because I think it's less work for me. But something about him seemed strange."[14]

Though Cristina didn't initially act on her intuition, she remembered it later and was the first person to thwart Reid's attempted suicide mission. I'm guessing that the tooth mark scar on Cristina's hand will continue to remind her in the future to act more quickly on her intuition.

The Israeli Model

In addition to checking all passengers—both physically and intuitively—El Al follows a number of security measures that are not regularly performed by U.S. airlines. For example, Israeli armed security guards are at all airport check-in counters, and they also inspect all vehicles that are permitted near El Al airplanes.

More Loopholes

In the 1996 film "Executive Decision," guns were placed in the food carts for terrorists who would be on board.

Halle Berry plays a brave stew who hides the passenger list, so the terrorists won't find the air marshal. Later she helps to land the plane, too.

When box cutters, like those used by the terrorists on 9-11, were later found on a number of planes, it was easy to imagine that they might have been placed on board by cleaning or catering staff. Cleaning and catering staff are not airline employees. They are contract personnel. And at many airports today, cleaning and catering staff do not pass through any security. I wish it weren't so.

Questionable Measures

I am very uncomfortable with a so-called "aircraft defensive measure" put forward by some pilots. These pilots are recommending that, at the first sign of a terrorist, the pilots should depressurize the plane and start a rapid descent.

No thank you! Depressurization can break the necks of passengers and stews. Anyone without a seatbelt will hit the ceiling.

Depressurization can also cause long-term problems to the ears, lungs, and hearts of passengers and cabin crews—but not to pilots, who have oxygen on tap in the cockpit.

Terrorism Strategy ★11. **For Legislators**
Check out www.skirsch.com for "Safe Mode" and other excellent ideas for security developed by millionaire entrepreneur Steve Kirsch.

The worst idea I've heard came from a reader who suggests that all seats should lock passengers in like the rides at amusement parks. Nah.

Cockpit Doors

Cockpit doors are now bullet-, heat-, and shock-proof at a cost of about $2 hundred million—paid by the U.S. taxpayer. The new doors have numeric pads on the outside.

If stews want in, they punch a code, a pilot gets up and looks out the peep-hole, then opens the door. If both pilots are incapacitated, stews can get in.

New cockpit security regulations on U.S. carriers require that when a pilot wants to use the lavatory, two flight attendants must leave their work and their passengers. One remains inside the cockpit, and the other stands outside the cockpit with a food cart blocking the cockpit door until that pilot is safely back inside the cockpit.

The two stews are to defend the cockpit, armed only with their smiles and their guile.

Terrorism Strategy ★12. **Whiff it**

This is unusual, but please hear me out. While jostling among other passengers, sniff the air. It has come out that all the 9-11 terrorists, as part of their suicide ritual, wore fragrance.[15] If you smell what appears to you to be an inappropriate fragrance on somebody, let the authorities know. Also—thoughtful air travelers avoid wearing scented personal products, such as hair spray, lotions, perfumes, and after shave. If you wear a scent for any amount of time, you will forfeit some of your sense of smell due to a natural blocking process of the brain.

Terrorists In Cockpits

Airline pilots have lobbied for guns on the grounds that this will make it safer for passengers. I believe there is another reason.

It is hush-hush among airline insiders that some of the 9-11 terrorists were actually inside the cockpits of the doomed planes before takeoff.[16]

How did the 9-11 terrorists get into the cockpits prior to takeoff?

They could have been invited in. Prior to 9-11, *any* pilot with *any* airline pilot ID could fly for free on *any* airline *any* time as long as there was an empty seat in the cockpit—no uniform needed.

There is usually at least one empty seat. The only time the seat is not available is in the rare event of a "check flight"—when management observes the flight crew.

After 9-11, many airlines discontinued this privilege for off-duty pilots. Other airlines now leave it up to the captain on each flight, as a large percentage of pilots commute to work, hitching rides in cockpits of their own and other airlines.

Since most commercial pilots have a military background, they have insisted on carrying guns so they won't be sitting ducks as they were on 9-11.

U.S. pilots got permission to pack loaded pistols on 11/25/02. Now, potentially 100,000 U.S. commercial pilots are carrying guns.

Rising From The Ashes

Certain themes recur in literature, and one of these is that ashes symbolize leaving behind the old and beginning anew. Here are three examples.

In the Bible, Job sat in a pile of ashes, mourning the loss of his family and struggling to understand the tragedy that had become his life. Then Jehovah restored Job's fortune and family.

In a classic children's story, Cinderella led a bitter life and, as her name implies, was covered in ashes (cinders) from the hearth while caring for her step-family. Then Prince Charming came along, and she was transformed into a spotless beauty.

In the ancient world, the ash metaphor is embodied in the phoenix, a giant bird with shining golden feathers. The mythological phoenix cyclically incinerated itself, then rose from its own ashes—reborn and renewed.

Across the ancient world, there are dozens of legends about the phoenix. A single feather of the phoenix was said to have dropped on Persia, creating the beginnings of culture. In Egypt, the phoenix symbolized the transmigration of the soul.

Another version from Japan, which inspires me now, depicts a phoenix rising from its own ashes with rainbow trails and gusts of fresh, sweet air wafting behind it.

The Ashes Of 9-11

After the tragic events of 9-11, we watched on TV as the New York Fire Department sifted through the ashes of the World Trade Center.

For many of us, our initial panic turned into soul searching as we observed the unfolding events. *How am I ever going to trust anyone again? What would I be doing with my life if I had all the choices in the world? Who am I, really?*

In my own life, fierce challenges that have shaken me to my knees have also brought me closer to being the person that I've always wanted to be—weaving into the fabric of my life the hope and inspiration that sustain me now.

58

In the chaos and pain of 9-11, many of us began to rethink our lives. It is my hope now that, through an informed public, safe and healthy flying will rise out of the ashes of 9-11 like the mythical phoenix. Ð

References
[1] www.washingtonpost.com, "Bombing," 1/27/02.
[2] www.bbc.com, "Final phone calls," 9/13/01.
[3] *Newsweek*, "Final moments #93," 9/22/01.
[4] "Delta flight attendant," excerpt, 9/14/01.
[5] HBO, "New York City 9/11/01," 5/26/02.
[6] *TIME*, 11/7/69.
[7] FAA, *Sourcebook of Criminal Justice*, 1987.
[8] *University Wire* (Syracuse, NY), 10/29/01.
[9] *San Francisco Chronicle*, "A trial run?" 1/6/02.
[10] *Florida Sun-Sentinel*, "Passengers," 12/23/01.
[11] www.scotlandonsunday.com, "Bomb," 12/01.
[12] www.imdb.com, Internet Movie Data Base.
[13] The O'Reilly Factor, Fox TV, 2/14/02.
[14] *TIME*, "Courage in the air," 9/9/02.
[15] www.abcnews.com, "Atta's note," 10/28/01.
[16] *New Hampshire News*, "Arm pilots," 9/26/01.

Terrorism Strategy ★13. **Affirmation**
Say over and over to yourself: I am guided and protected. I am safe and unaffected. Perfect.

Streaking

Wise Passenger Quiz

Which statement is correct? "Streaking" in aviation vernacular refers to:

a) Naked passengers running through airplane cabins.

b) A part of the jet stream known as "vapor trails."

c) Flushed material on 767s.

d) A featured portion of TWA flight #800's court record.

Answer

All these statements are correct answers. Let me tell you why.

A) Naked Passengers

On March 10, 1974, James Todwin streaked on a Pan Am 707 between New York and London. Todwin ran 100 percent buff naked and uninhibited up the aisle from the back of the economy cabin into a first class bathroom.

The story I heard from other crews was that the streaker had stashed his clothing under the sink in a first-class lavatory and that all the passengers thought it was hilarious—it really made the flight go faster. After the incident, the stews gave the rather good-looking James and his two friends a free bottle of champagne.

It Was Hip, Man

During the 1970s, streaking anywhere was hip. But like a summer tan line, streaking faded in the autumn of the counter-culture fad. Many of today's jets were, in fact, manufactured in the 70s. But today, along with retrofitted recirculated air, all planes now have more seats, and narrower aisles.

In the good old days, a stew could walk up any aisle without bumping passengers. With today's narrow aisles, plump flight attendants (now that they've done away with weight check) have to work in first class or in a galley, and thigh bruises mark all stews, who now have to wiggle up and down the aisles. I would venture to say that streaking up a narrow aisle today—without colliding into feet and elbows—is virtually impossible.

B) A Part Of The Jet Stream

The jet stream contains what is known as "jet streaks." Made from vapor trails of winds, jet streaks speed faster than surrounding winds.[1]

C) Flushed Material On 767s

According to manufacturing sources, flushed material from the aft lavatories on 767s streaks through pipes over the heads of passengers at 90 mph to a holding tank in the front of the plane. Pilots talk about this in the form of a riddle: "What part of the 767 has the fastest ground speed?"

D) TWA #800

TWA #800 crashed off the coast of Long Island, New York (7/96). Many eyewitnesses said they saw a streak of light hit the plane before it exploded.

For example, Major Meyer, who was on a training mission in a military transport plane at the time, said he first saw the streak, and then TWA #800 was "blown to smithereens."[2]

There were hundreds of other eyewitnesses. Check it out on the Internet: TWA +800 +streak.

Some people are convinced that TWA #800 was shot down by shoulder-fired missiles or bombs from terrorists.

There's also a conspiracy theory that the streak was caused by U.S. Navy missiles, then covered up. Still others speculate that TWA #800 was hit by a meteor.

The federal investigation into the in-flight breakup over the Atlantic Ocean of TWA #800 took four years—and is reported to have cost taxpayers 40 million dollars.

The National Transportation Safety Board determined that the probable cause was an explosion in a fuel tank on the wing. The source of the explosion was not determined, nor did the investigation pinpoint the cause of the streak.

212 passengers, 4 pilots, and 14 flight attendants lost their lives on TWA #800.

Streaking Today

Streaking today just isn't what it used to be. In 2000, a 23-year-old Frenchman removed all of his clothing for some unknown reason during the safety demonstration prior to takeoff. The flight was subsequently delayed in Athens while the man was escorted off the plane[3]—the account does not tell if he disembarked in an airplane blanket, or if the authorities waited for him to dress.

In 2001, a 36-year-old Texan stripped between Los Angeles and Beijing. Nobody seemed to mind until the man tried to open an exit door in flight. Then the plane diverted to Anchorage to drop off the "unruly" passenger.[4]

It's clear that the people who are streaking today are not doing it just for kicks like in the more carefree days of the 70s. In the old days, we stews gave streakers champagne, but today all they get is an escort right off the plane.

Flying Nude In The Future

By the time you take off your shoes, belt, and jacket at security, so you can walk through without a blip, some people feel they might just as well take it all off. Crew members are already joking around about flying naked: "Fight terrorism. Fly naked."

I believe that journalist Ann Coulter was the first to bring up the subject of flying nude, only a week after the World Trade Center disaster:

"Unless the government is going to require passengers and crew to travel naked with no luggage, there is no spot search devisable that can keep the skies safe."[5]

In Your Dreams

While working on this chapter, I received this naked-appropriate horoscope from astrologer, Rob Brezsny, which seemed to open an interesting and creative context to the enigma of streaking on airliners:

"Chances are good you'll dream of being naked in public sometime soon. Such a dream will signify your readiness—indeed, your urgent need—to reveal more of who you really are in your waking life."[6] ☽

"Streaking" Strategy ★1. Thou shalt not streak on airplanes—in your waking life.

References

[1] *USA Today*, "Jetstream and weather," 12/31/96.

[2] AP (New York), "TWA 800," 7/17/95

[3] *Ananova*, "Man strips on plane," 3/12/01.

[4] *Anchorage News*, "Passenger strips," 8/15/01.

[5] Coulter, Ann, "Capitol Hill Blues," 9/23/01.

[6] www.freewillastrology.com/newsletter.

Medical Strategy ★1. **Disclosure**

If you have a heart condition and you fear the possibility of cardiac arrest or illness on an airplane, it may be best not to fly alone. If you do fly alone, it would be good to alert your crew. Careful—only speak to your stew after takeoff. If you paint too dire a picture before takeoff (to stews or ticket agents), your airline may refuse to take you.

Medical Strategy ★2. **Time to Fly**

If you have had a heart attack or a stroke within the last 30 days, or if you have heart disease or any condition that weakens the heart, speak to your doctor before flying. You may want to postpone your trip until you are stronger, due to the changes in air pressure and reduced oxygen on board.

Cardiac Arrest
& Medical Emergencies

"I have a heart condition and am planning to fly soon. What if I have a heart attack on the airplane? The plane can't land at an emergency room. Is it safe for me to fly?"

Having a heart attack on an airliner can be a terrifying experience.

Luckily, most planes now carry defibrillators. In this chapter, you will learn on which flights you can expect to find defibrillators and how to use them.

I cannot tell you whether or not it is safe for *you* to fly. What I will do is explain to you how medical emergencies are handled on planes, and offer you an in depth look at all the medical supplies available on board.

My hope is to educate you sufficiently so that you will feel comfortable making your own risk assessment about whether or not you should fly. After reading this chapter you will also be better able to discuss your flight plans with your doctor.

Restart The Heart

Defibrillators are one of the miracles of modern technology. Even when a person has stopped breathing and has no pulse, a defibrillator can get the heart beating properly again.

Defibrillators are about the size of a laptop computer. Though all U.S. airlines are required to have defibrillators by May 2004, defibrillators are not a "no-go" item—in other words, if a defibrillator is not on board, the plane will still take off.

So, essentially, there is no guarantee that you will find a defibrillator on any given flight.

Shout For The Defibrillator

An estimated 350,000 Americans are struck by cardiac arrest each year, and the survival rate is 90 percent when a defibrillator is used during the first few minutes.

Speed is of the essence. For every minute that it is delayed, survival rates actually drop about 10 percent, according to the FAA.

So, on board, if someone appears to be having a heart attack, it is vital to get help immediately.

Medical Strategy ★3. **Ring & Shout**

If you experience pain in your heart and you suspect it is cardiac arrest, ring your call button repeatedly and shout to other passengers, "Hurry! Ask the flight attendant to bring the defibrillator immediately to seat # ___!" (It will save time if you give the seat number.)

How To Use The Defibrillator

Defibrillators are to be used on board only when a passenger is unconscious, without a pulse, and not breathing.

The machine provides an electrocardiogram to guide your stew or a physician who may be a passenger on the flight.

Defibrillators even tell them where to put the pads to shock the heart back into beating. The defibrillator can correct mistakes, too—if handled incorrectly, the defibrillator will over-ride any mistakes.

These defibrillators are packaged with latex-free gloves, a razor, scissors, and a battery.

Legal Action Brings Defibrillators

A 1998 lawsuit in Boston's federal court opened the way for defibrillators on commercial airliners.

The estate of a 37-year-old passenger who died of cardiac arrest between Boston and San Francisco brought an action against a U.S. airline for failing to provide equipment and medicine for the treatment of an in-flight heart attack.

The case was settled out of court, and since then, all U.S. airlines have agreed, one by one, to carry defibrillators. This example shows how a good change in aviation safety can come about after one person initiates a legal action.

A final note about the onboard defibrillators. If the captain has a heart attack, the defibrillator cannot be used in the cockpit as it could interfere with the aircraft's instrumentation.

Emergency Medical Kits

By law, U.S. airlines must provide specific medical supplies to passengers. These supplies are stowed throughout the aircraft in a variety of "kits" —First-aid Kit, Sharps Container Kit, Infection Control Kit, and Emergency Medical Kit.

The Emergency Medical Kit is a "no-go" item—the plane will not take off without one.

The Emergency Medical Kit is cocooned in plastic wrap and also sealed. A green seal indicates that the kit has never been used. Yellow means the kit has been used but can be used again. Red means the kit should not be used.

This kit includes endotracheal tubes, blood pressure meter, stethoscope, needles, syringes, thermometers, scissors, tourniquets, resuscitator micro shields, and catheters.

There are also a dozen or so allopathic drugs in this kit, such as epinephrine for asthma and dextrose for insulin shock. There are sedatives, too, for passengers in pain.

Sedatives from the kit have been used to subdue berserk passengers and even a captured terrorist.

70

Medical Strategy ★4. **Drink Water**

Keep hydrated when you fly because the cabin air is very dry. Dehydration can make us more vulnerable to many ills. Prevent dehydration by drinking at least 8 ounces of water for every hour of travel—from home until after landing. Caffeinated beverages can exacerbate dehydration, so if you drink coffee and sodas, drink extra water, too.

Tranquilizing the "Shoe Bomber"

After the "shoe bomber" was caught (12/01), he was injected with a sedative, according to the news. I assumed that this sedative came from the Emergency Medical Kit, but I wanted to fact-check, so I asked the FAA. The FAA was secretive. They told me, "You have to ask the FBI."

The FBI was secretive, too. "This is now out of our jurisdiction," the FBI told me. "You have to ask the Department of Justice."

The Department of Justice told me, "We are not saying, at this point, if the tranquilizer came from the in-flight medical kit."

But then, luckily, I found confirmation on bbc.com: "Two doctors who were among the passengers administered a sedative from the airliner's medical kit."[1]

Good Samaritans

The Emergency Medical Kit has equipment and drugs that can only be dispensed by medical professionals who may be on board as passengers.

To find a medical professional, cabin crews will look over the Passenger List, and they may also make an announcement: "Ladies and gentlemen, is there a medical professional on board?"

A qualified medical professional includes anyone who is licensed to provide medical care, such as doctors, nurses, paramedics, emergency medical technicians, acupuncturists, naturopaths, and physician assistants.

On any given flight, however, there is no guarantee that there will be a medical professional who has not been drinking. These good samaritans are not on duty on board. They are simply volunteers who happen to be traveling.

The good samaritan/medical professional is not necessarily well rested, either, when treating passengers and prescribing drugs. Nor is there a guarantee that you will be fortunate enough to find a medical professional who is trained in "altitude physiology." Personally, I am wary of the side effects of drugs and only like to take them judiciously.

In 1998, the Aviation Medical Assistance Act removed liability for both the airlines and good samaritan volunteers, unless willful misconduct could be proven.

I Advocate Protection For Stews, Too

Oddly, stews are not covered by the 1998 liability law that protects good samaritan passengers and the airlines.[2]

The FAA and Congress were actually petitioned to remove liability for stews, too, and for some unfathomable reason, they refused.

As it stands now, if a medical professional does not happen to be a passenger on your flight and you become ill, your flight attendant, wishing to help, actually puts herself in jeopardy.

In spite of this, the airlines expect stews to care for ill and injured passengers. In annual courses for cabin crew, the airlines provide medical training that includes how to handle defibrillators, how to deliver babies, how to offer CPR, and how to administer first-aid treatments for dozens of contingencies—from burns to broken bones.

Medical Strategy ★5. **Rest Stops**

If you have a chronic health condition, schedule rest stops after about 7 hours of flight.

Medical Strategy ★6. **Sleep**

Get plenty of sleep for several days before you fly to ensure that you will be rested when you embark on your journey.

Flying ERs

On most flights when there is a medical emergency, the chief purser advises the captain if an unscheduled landing is recommended. Another option to which some airlines subscribe is to have the purser consult with a ground-based ER using the in-flight phone; then the ER decides if a good samaritan's care is sufficient, if there is one, or if the airplane should make an unscheduled landing.

According to MedAire, the company that provides the ERs, in 2002 the number of calls for in-flight medical assistance was over 8,000.[3]

About 10 percent of the calls were "cardiac" related, and another 10 percent were "respiratory." In addition, over 21 percent of the in-flight requests for assistance involved "fainting" passengers.

I believe the predominant reason passengers are having cardiac, respiratory, and fainting spells on planes today is because there simply isn't enough oxygen. Recirculated air, full of carbon dioxide, just doesn't cut it—even for people in their prime.

Medical Strategy ★7. **For Congress**
Authorize studies on medical emergencies in flight, as well as flight-related medical problems among frequent flyers, crew, and the elderly— noting the aircraft type and the airline.

Vital Signs In The Air

An important new technology has been developed for handling in-flight medical emergencies, but is it now available on only a few carriers.

Special "in-flight medical monitors" can actually read a passenger's vital signs right at their seat, then transmit them, using any in-flight phone, to a ground-based physician.

In April 2003, the transmission of a passenger's vital sign data was used successfully for the first time from the air to diagnose and treat a heart attack on an international flight.

Transmitting vital signs from the plane offers passengers with medical emergencies the attention they need in real time, thus greatly improving onboard care and saving the airlines money, too, because they can more effectively determine the level of the emergency, which helps them to reduce unscheduled landings. Airlines claim that unscheduled landings can cost up to $80,000 with extra fuel and landing fees.

The in-flight medical monitors are capable of reporting a person's blood pressure, pulse rate, temperature, electrocardiogram (ECG), blood oxygen, and carbon dioxide levels.[4]

Once the monitors are on all planes, the airlines will of course have a harder time denying the low levels of oxygen and high levels of carbon dioxide in commercial jet cabins.

Infection Control Kit

The Infection Control Kit contains material that looks like kitty litter with a similarly absorbent nature. It is used on board to help prevent the spread of infections by soaking up bodily fluids.

Anything on board that has come in contact with bodily fluids (pillows, blankets) is to be placed in the Infection Control Kit.

The kit contains a plastic scoop and latex gloves for handling contaminated items, and it has plastic bags with ties and labels, and disinfectant wipes.

The flight attendant manual says that flight attendants "are at minimal risk of exposure to potentially infectious diseases." But if a passenger with HIV-Aids becomes ill or wounded, a stew could become infected by bodily fluids through any break in her skin, even a skin rash.

Common sense tells us that any stew with a rash or wound should be grounded.

A Question About Air Sickness

From a reader (8/02): "My grandson was sick on a flight and vomited, soiling the blanket across his knees. I called an attendant and requested that she remove the blanket so that he could stand up and go to the washroom. She did not remove it, and I had to ask her a second time about 10 minutes later. She then put the blanket into a plastic bag, but left the bag by his seat. Finally, I asked another attendant to move the bag. She said, 'We can't do it now.' I was angry by then and told her in no uncertain terms that she was to do whatever it took to remove the bag. She finally did. But why did it take her so long?"

Answer: In order for attendants to handle anything that has bodily fluids on it, they must deal with it in a very specific way. First, they have to locate the sealed Infection Control Kit, which, on some planes, might even be stowed in an overhead bin under some pillows.

Then, so that stews don't touch anything that may be contaminated with contagious diseases, they have to put on latex gloves and use forceps to pick up the potentially contaminated item.

A soiled blanket, for example, has to be placed in a specially marked "hazardous waste bag," sealed up, and stowed in a closed-off lavatory. A report must then be written in the ship's log so ground cleaning staff will be alerted to the special handling needed for their protection.

During some phases of the flight, especially when serving drinks and food, stews are juggling many tasks. Having done this myself for two decades, all I can say is you have to trust they will decide what is the best priority for all concerned. On your flight, there may have been other urgent responsibilities they had to attend to.

Sharps Container Kit

The Sharps Container Kit consists of a bio-hazard bag with a clamp, a red plastic container, anti-microbial and disinfectant wipes, and gloves for handling needles, broken glass, etc.

A colleague of mine was on a flight where a diabetic fainted, then was given an insulin shot by a physician/passenger. The needle was left haphazardly on the passenger's tray table, and when my friend picked it up to dispose of it, it pricked her skin. She then had to get a Hepatitis B shot and an AIDS test. Luckily, both tests were negative.

On board, needles should always be disposed of in the Sharps Container Kit. This is supposed to be done by the physician or by the passenger who self-administers a shot, such as a diabetic.

First-Aid Kit

The onboard First-aid Kit has rubber gloves, scissors, ammonia inhalants, antiseptic swabs, resuscitation mask, splints, bandages, and burn ointment.

When I was flying, this was the only kit we carried.

When actress/model Lauren Hutton was on my flight leaving Bangkok with a bad burn on her leg from a motorcycle accident, I dressed her wound with the burn ointment and bandages from our aircraft's First-aid Kit.

> ## Medical Strategy ★8. **Bless this Trip**
> Before takeoff, pray: May the pilots, stews, and passengers on this plane be blessed. I give thanks, and do my best. I have faith that the Almighty Pilot takes care of the rest.

As it turned out, Ms. Hutton decided to disembark at a transit stop prior to her scheduled stop because she was having so much discomfort.

She told me she was concerned because she had no cash. She wanted cash to pay for a taxi to a hotel, where she would then have money wired to her. I loaned her a few hundred dollars from my purser fund—this against company regulations, but what the heck—and I took her personal check.

The number of First-aid Kits on board depends on the number of seats. Planes with less than 51 seats have one kit. Up to 151 seats, 2 kits. Up to 251 seats, 3 kits. Any more, 4 First-aid Kits—so there should always be a First-aid Kit, if you need it, relatively close to your seat. ℘

References

[1] www.bbc.com, "Plane bomb plot," 12/23/01.
[2] *FAA Federal Register,* V 66-71, 4/12/01.
[3] www.medaire.com.
[4] www.rdtltd.com.

"Tall" Strategy ★1. **Doctor's Note**

Ask your doctor to write a letter requesting adequate room for your long legs, then show your note when you check in at the airport. Also, have your note handy during boarding, and if there is time, show your note to a flight attendant. Ask her to let you know if a seat with adequate legroom opens up. Your plight is obvious, but it can help if you speak up.

"Tall" Strategy ★2. **Airline Employees**

If you want a special favor from airline employees (such as a better seat), be friendly, use humor, but first and foremost, acknowledge how busy they are. Perhaps say: I see how very busy you are and my heart goes out to you. I'm in kind of a situation here. My leg bone is longer than the legroom on the plane. I don't know if there is anything you can, do but I wanted you to be aware of my situation.

Too Tall

"My father, a tall man in his 70s, flies twice a year from the Midwest to Hawaii to visit me. The flights are long, he is cramped on the plane, then he always arrives with a backache. Do you think he should request an exit row or a bulkhead?"

Your father can certainly request the exit row if he feels up to the responsibility that goes with it. Exit-row passengers are expected to help the crew when there is an emergency. Specifically, they are to help other passengers disembark through their exits before leaving the plane themselves.

This chapter provides tall passengers with information on how best to get an exit-row seat. In addition, you will find a number of other strategies for coping with the special demands of flying when you are too tall to fit in an airplane seat.

This chapter speaks up for the plight of tall passengers, and also for others who may not fit the airline mold for a variety of reasons.

Exit Rows

Very few passengers are lucky enough to get exit-row seats because there are so few exits on each plane (from 2 to 12 depending on the aircraft).

Exit rows usually have a lot of extra legroom; this is so passengers can get out of the plane quickly during emergency situations.

"Tall" Strategy ★3. **Exit Rows**

To get an exit row, arrive at the airport early. At the check-in counter, stand up straight, look pleadingly, and let the ticket agent know that you have memorized all the exit-row responsibilities. These are: before takeoff, you will make sure the exit area is free of luggage. If an emergency evacuation begins, you will first look out your exit to see that the area is safe (no fire). Next, you will open the exit, then help others to disembark before disembarking yourself. If you manage to get an exit row (whew!) and you have a connecting flight, ask the ticket agent if it's possible to reserve your exit-row seat for both flights.

"Tall" Strategy ★4. **False Exit Rows**

The exit row designation often applies to seats one row *ahead* of the actual exit. These seats have even less than normal legroom. So if you get an exit row, be sure it is an exit row.

"Tall" Strategy ★5. **Sign Up**

Get a frequent flyer account with one airline and be eligible for "economy plus," with more legroom and also frequent flyers favors, such as exit rows and upgrades.

Bulkheads

Bulkheads are the walls in front of each section. For example, 747s have 5 bulkheads on the main deck, plus one more upstairs.

Bulkheads aren't perfect, though. Some bulkheads are too close so you don't have adequate room for your feet to slide forward. And on many planes, the armrests in that row don't come up.

However, at least no one will recline into your knees at the bulkhead, and it's also easier to get in and out of your seat so you can stand up for exercise and stretching.

Basketball Players

How do basketball players manage on planes when they fly to "away" games?

To start with, professional athletes usually fly first class. But if players have to fly in economy, they get two seats because the only way their legs will fit in economy is sideways.

Three seats are preferable—then the player can sit in the middle and switch his legs left and right during the flight.

A better solution is when basketball teams charter airplanes. Players can then push down the seatbacks in front of them, and prop up their legs.

Ahhhh. If only we could all do that.

Many teams have purchased planes and re-configured them with plenty of stretch-out room.

"Tall" Strategy ★6. **Commuter Planes**

Some commuter planes have an extra seat in the last row where the aisle would be. This seat might not be on the seating chart, but ask for it. You have the entire aisle for your legs.

"Tall" Strategy ★7. **Avoid Peak Travel**

When making your reservation, ask for help in finding the "least crowded flights" because you are over 6-feet tall.

"Tall" Strategy ★8. **Preboard**

Preboard. If an airline employee wants to know why you are preboarding say: My legs are long; I need to make sure my bags are stowed in overhead bins to maximize the legroom.

Correspondence With Talls

I get a lot of mail from tall passengers. Their letters break my heart because their special needs are virtually ignored, causing a tremendous amount of pain and suffering.

For the most part, these gentle giants know that arguments with airline employees won't get you anywhere.

Arguing with crew can only lead to trouble. In 2003, even rock star Courtney Love was arrested after being "verbally abusive" to a stew.[1]

"Procrustean Bed" In The Sky

Flying in economy is torture for talls. Airline seats are for talls what the procrustean bed was for travelers in the mythology of ancient Greece. The story goes that Procrustes had a bed & breakfast near Athens. It was a sinister place; the beds never fit, so Procrustes cut off the legs of his tall guests.

The dictionary defines "procrustean" as "aiming to produce uniformity by violent methods" and the procrustean bed has become proverbial for ruthlessly forcing people to fit into an unnatural standard.

Flying is a perfect example of the procrustean standard. The airlines arbitrarily insist we must all fit into their sardine seats regardless of the length of our bones. Talls don't get their legs cut off—only their circulation.

"Tall" Strategy ★9. **Stretching**

Stretch before, during, and after flight to help your muscles prepare and recover.

"Tall" Strategy ★10. **Get Up**

You don't have to stay in your seat unless the seat belt sign is on. Be smart—get up and walk around, or even stand by the exit door and do knee bends.

Tall Tales

A 2003 Apple laptop commercial shows a very tall passenger seated in a first-class aisle seat on a 767—he is so tall he opens the overhead bin without standing up. 767 overhead bins are especially low; so are the doorways. Talls need to remember to duck when embarking and disembarking.

For those over 6-feet tall, there are many foibles, hazards, hardships, and indignities of flying. Here are excerpts from letters I've received from talls over the last seven years:

• "When the person in front of me reclined, it crushed my kneecaps. I've had $100,000 of surgery on those knees, so I'm kind of protective."

• "The only way I could fit in the aisle seat was with my right leg extending slightly into the aisle. After we were airborne, I awoke with a sharp pain in my knee. The flight attendant had hit my foot with the beverage cart, bending my foot back and spraining my knee."

"Tall" Strategy ★11. **The One in Front**

If the person in front of you reclines into your knees, get up and stand tall in front of him, and with a warm smile, explain your problem. Ask for their consideration. When all else fails, offer them an incentive.

• "It is impossible to see out of airplane windows without deforming my great posture. The windows on most planes are too low for me. I am a geologist and would rather look outside at the great geology than talk to my seat neighbor—unless it was someone as good looking as you! My ideal plane would have a dome in the floor so we could see everything."

• "In window seats, I get claustrophobic attacks due to the curving wall next to me."

• "The back of my head easily goes over the top of the seat. This leaves me with a concern that the airlines are not adequately providing for my safety because, in severe turbulence, my head is not supported at all."

• "The restroom problems would be hilarious if not so precarious. At my height, and male, I have to stand slanted in the restroom and cock my head far to one side while trying to urinate."

• "I was awakened by an ear-piercing scream. My 6' 4" husband beside me was in agony because the person in front had reclined and the metal supports for the tray went directly into my husband's knees!"

• "One night flight, my knees were jammed against the bulkhead. I stood up and leaned against the wall for 7 hours. I had just completed a high dose treatment for Multiple Sclerosis relapse and was quite ill."

"Tall" Strategy ★12. **Blood Clots**
Check your legs for injuries after flying. If there is swelling, pain, or redness indicative of deep vein thrombosis, attend to the healing your body requires.

• "I literally couldn't get into my assigned seat without jamming my legs. Shortly after my return home, I suffered a deep vein thrombosis, then almost died from a pulmonary embolism."

• "I've designed a little graphite reinforced plastic device that I can put together which prevents the seat in front from reclining. It's my 'knee saver'."

Choosing An Airline

There is no general consensus among talls regarding which airlines are the most thoughtful and on which carriers they get the worst treatment.

I think this is because the way talls are often treated boils down to what any airline employee feels like doing—or is capable of doing—for a tall passenger on a given day.

One tall reader told me that a flight attendant came up to him after takeoff and said, "I'll do something for you because you look like you're in pain," and she moved him to first class.

Don't expect this. Most of the time, flight attendants are caught between a rock and a hard place. On every flight, stews have more tasks than they can possibly complete, so they prioritize as best they they can, i.e., this person is sick, equipment is broken, short staffing, berserk passengers, one thing or another.

Occasionally, a check-in agent will offer an upgrade without charge to a tall passenger. Please be aware that employees who choose to bend the rules for compassion's sake take a personal risk, since supervisors generally stick to the airline party line, which as I know it, has no room for compassion.

Today's airline policies dictate that airline employees tell tall passengers who can't fit in the seats, it's just tough luck, sit there anyway.

Something has to change. People have to travel by air for business and personal reasons, and many times there is no equivalent ground or sea transportation available. On top of this, most people simply cannot afford first class or business class.

Choosing Specific Seats

The heirarchy of legroom on planes starts with first class, then business class, then the exit rows in economy, and finally, economy plus.

The worst seats on board are in economy, also known as "Y class" by the airlines, and "sardine class" and "misery class" by passengers.

"Tall" Strategy ★13. **Take Care**

To help diminish your flying discomforts, take care of yourself the best you can after flying. Bring what you'll need to relax and treat your muscles (such as herbal balms and teas). On board, wear loose clothing so as not to constrict circulation, drink plenty of good water, avoid alcohol and airline meals, and try to make friends with the cabin crew—you may need them as allies.

Sometimes, passengers ask me for specific rows they can request at check-in, but there are no best seat numbers. Each airline bolts in its own seats, and the rows rearrange easily to make more or less spacing. So the same seat number on a flight today could have less legroom a week from now.

To make matters more complex, the row configurations change with each aircraft type, and connecting flights often have aircraft changes.

Speaking With Once Voice

From a reader (1/02): "As a community of tall people, do we have legal grounds to demand a seat on an airplane that fits? I'm 6' 5" and I just can't fit in an airplane seat. Do you think the airlines are aware of the situation for tall passengers?"

Answer: Of course the airlines are aware of the plight of tall passengers. It is my hope now, though, that in this climate where the airlines are reorganizing, a window of opportunity will open and some smart airlines will see the advantage of treating talls fairly.

Hundreds of frequent-flying tall passengers have written to me, so I feel sure the business is there for smart airlines. A caring gesture at this level would certainly impress all passengers, regardless of their physique.

I look forward to the day when it is not necessary to be litigious with the airlines. There is at least one legal precedent, though. In 2002, a tall passenger was awarded a small settlement for being forced to endure an "agonizing 8-hour flight."[2]

Meanwhile, talls may want to deluge their legislators with letters. Please CC me. And fly first class when you can—that's as good as it gets. Ð

"Tall" Strategy ★14. **For Airlines**
Configure all planes with adequate legroom.

References

[1] www.cnn.com, "Courtney Love arrested," 2/4/03.
[2] www.bbc.co.uk, "Tall passenger wins," 1/24/02.

—Jill Engledow, The Maui News

"My theory about long-distance air flight is like the one people sometimes cite about childbirth: one is willing to go back and do it again only because one forgets how painful the experience is. As it happens, Diana Fairechild also likens air flight to childbirth, but in her simile the passenger is like the baby and the jet the womb which, unlike mom's, fails to adequately sustain the well-being of its inhabitants."

Fairechild's Passenger Bill of Rights

No bill protecting airline passengers has passed into law as this book goes to press, though several versions of an airline passenger bill of rights have been introduced in the U.S. Congress and talked about by the media for at least four years.

In my opinion, even if one of the proposed Congressional bills had passed, it would not have gone far enough in safeguarding the rights of airline passengers.

The bills that have been proposed focused primarily on convenience issues, such as providing prompt ticket refunds and finding out why your plane is delayed, rather than on vital safety issues, such as ensuring that the airlines provide adequate oxygen and water for everyone onboard.

For over a decade, I have been lobbying many governments around the world, the airlines, the flying public, and the media about the hazards of air travel that are directly related to airline policies —the pesticides, noise, recirculated air, radiation, and contaminated water, air, and cabin furnishings. These hazards of air travel violate our right to life.

I now present for the first time "Fairechild's Passenger Bill of Rights"—the ten most important airline safety issues that I feel must immediately be addressed by the airlines and their partners in government.

The **Bill Of Rights**

The original U.S. Bill of Rights was ratified in 1791. These rights form the first 10 amendments to the United States Constitution, and they list the inherent rights of U.S. citizens. The Bill of Rights guarantees U.S. citizens freedom of speech, freedom of expression, and much more.

The founders of the United States created the Bill of Rights to protect its citizens from any potential oppressive use of government power.

Thomas Jefferson, whose Natural Rights Theory inspired the Bill of Rights, wrote, "A bill of rights is what the people are entitled to against every government on earth, general or particular, and what no just government should refuse."

As a result of the Bill of Rights' restraint on government, the United States has been seen all over the world as a place of refuge and hope.

In the 1942 film "Casablanca," the airplane symbolized this hope. At the beginning of the film, we see downtown Casablanca, with its cafes lining the streets. The camera zooms in as we see refugees from war-torn Europe trying, in whatever way they can, to flee to the United States.

Next, we hear the motor hum of an airplane. As a DC3 flies across the sky, all refugees' eyes are skyward. "Perhaps tomorrow we will be on that plane," says a beautiful European refugee, as the music crescendos, full of hope.

Preemptions Override Protections

In the 1978 Airline Deregulation Act, the airlines were granted a federal "preemption" that permitted their airline regulations to override state consumer protection laws.

Now the airlines pollute the earth and the skies like nobody's business, and a consumer who has a claim against an airline has hardly any recourse under the laws that automatically apply to all other businesses. When the imbalance of power becomes this great, what might happen? Read on to find out what DID happen.

Passengers Without Rights

During a blizzard in Detroit (2/99), a number of large planes filled with passengers were held on the snowy tarmac for up to 11 hours!

After the first few hours, all food and drinks were used up, and toilet facilities were not working. Passengers, demanding to disembark, were told they would be arrested if they didn't return to their seats immediately.

Thus, passengers were denied their right to get off that dirty airplane—and even their right to speak. Northwest Airlines apparently could have towed the planes to a hangar to disembark these passengers. But, instead, the airline chose to save the towing fees and leave thousands of passengers all night long on dank planes.

Did the airline forget that passengers are human beings—and not cargo?

Approximately 3,700 passengers joined a class-action suit against Northwest for "forced imprisonment." They settled out of court for $1,000 to $2,000 apiece—a pittance compared to the consequences of such an ordeal.

Based on my two decades of flying, I am certain that the health of many passengers would have suffered greatly from this level of trauma.

Outraged passengers lobbied Congress. The rallying theme was: Passengers check only their luggage at the airport, not their rights as human beings.

Congress Considers

Congress held hearings and, in response to testimony given at those hearings, a bill was introduced to recognize airline passenger rights.

Then the Air Transport Association, a consortium of large airlines, promised Congress that the airlines would do better. So Congress decided that the airlines should be given the chance to take better care of passengers.

Thus was born (6/17/99) an agreement called the Airline Customer Service Commitment. It provided an escape from any new laws because the airlines volunteered to take better care of their passengers.

The airlines promised to improve service in several areas including being more responsive to customer complaints and handling "bumped" passengers (when your reservation is ignored and given to someone else) more fairly.

Over a year later, the Department of Transportation, usually the airlines' best friend, reported on the Commitment. The report prompted many to conclude that the airlines were just not capable of taking better care of passengers.

The picture of a grinning fox watching the hen house comes to mind.

More Bills In Congress

Additional passenger rights bills have subsequently been introduced in the U.S. Congress, but nothing has passed so far. Some of these bills are still winding their way through the political labyrinth today.

Most of the titles of this next generation of bills consist of various combinations of the words Airline, Air, or Aviation followed by either Passenger, Travelers, Consumer, or Customer and ending with Rights, Fair Treatment, Service Improvement, or Right to Know.

For the most part, these bills encompass a common core that includes all or most of the promises the airlines had already made but failed to fulfill in their 1999 Commitment.

97

Significantly, all the bills recognize that passengers have the right to exit a plane when it has been on the ground for a lengthy period.

Several of the new proposed bills demand disclosure for frequent flyer redemption points. One suggests a lost luggage tracking system. Another wants to eliminate penalties on roundtrip tickets.

A couple of the bills deal with medical care in the sky, and one even says that passengers have the right to know which insecticide is used on board—since I started that campaign in 1992 when I wrote about "disinsection" in **Jet Smart**, I am happy to see it has reached the halls of Congress.

My Fight For Passenger Rights

On the following pages, you will find my proposal for the ten most vital airline policy changes now needed to protect passengers.

For full and up-to-date details about the flying hazards introduced here, along with strategies on what you can do to take care of yourself in the meantime while we work toward changes in the aviation industry, please read the specific chapters on these subjects in various volumes throughout **The Jet Safe & Easy Series**.

You can also find a lot of information in **Jet Smarter** and on my web site. With my experience and my visionary eye, I see these rights ultimately enacted into laws that protect the flying public.

Article #1. Poison Protection

Spraying pesticide on airline passengers and throughout aircraft cabins must be stopped. If pesticide is used inside a plane, then the airline must be required to disclose every time that pesticide is applied. Along with this, the brand name of the pesticide and its symptoms of poisoning in humans (both mild and acute) must be made easily available to passengers.

Article #2. Fresh Air

Passengers must be provided the same quality air (percentage of oxygen) that pilots get—for more than two decades pilots have been getting more than ten times the amount of fresh air. Oxygen must be readily available on every flight to anyone suffering from hypoxia.

Article #3. Drinking Water

Potable drinking water must be provided on all commercial aircraft—at the very least, 8 ounces per hour per person. It is essential that crew and passengers consume adequate good-quality drinking water in order to prevent the many serious side effects of dehydration, such as deep vein thrombosis, fatigue, and brain fog (duh! what?).

Article #4. Smooth Turbulence

The airlines and their partners in government need to use high-tech measures to forecast whatever atmospheric conditions can toss about a jet in mid air. Technology to eliminate or at least vastly reduce clear air turbulence must now be made available to airlines. While we wait for the implementation of this technology, airlines should drop the euphemisms in emergency briefings and offer passengers solid information on how to protect themselves from turbulence-related injuries.

Article #5. Reduce Diseases

Cabin air contamination from contagious diseases must be treated as an airworthiness issue—if clean air is not delivered, then planes must be grounded. High efficiency air filters must be installed on all aircraft and checked before every flight. People with known airborne diseases should not be permitted to fly without a doctor's assurance that their illness is out of its contagious phase. The airlines must not be permitted to impose penalty charges on passengers who act responsibly when they change their reservations due to contagious diseases.

Article #6. Reduce Toxins

Air contamination by toxins must be treated as an airworthiness issue. If there is any suspicion of toxins in an airplane cabin, passengers and crew must be offered blood tests. Toxins can cause cancer, genetic mutations, and death. Sources of toxins in airplane cabins include, but are not limited to, hydraulic fluid leaks, engine oil leaks, jet fuel exhaust, and cabin furnishings.

Article #7. Aging Aircraft

The FAA must be restrained from issuing waivers of safety rules for aging aircraft. All past requests for exemptions must be made public. The age of every commercial airplane must be published and made readily available to passengers at airports before boarding.

Article #8. Safe Cargo

Hazardous materials and pharmaceutical grade germs and viruses must no longer be permitted as cargo on commercial jets. There is presently a great gap in security between air cargo and passenger operations. It's time to close this gap and make every aspect of aircraft operations safe for passengers.

Article #9. Safe Work Rules

Airline crew of U.S. companies and U.S. air marshals must be offered the same work rules that the government agency OSHA stipulates and enforces for work performed anywhere in the United States. The flying public relies on airline crew and air marshals for their safety, yet airline crews and air marshals now work twelve-, fourteen-, and even sixteen-hour shifts, while also suffering daily from oxygen deprivation, sleep deprivation, and the radical time zone shifts associated with jetlag. It is time to insure that aviation workers have safe working conditions for their own health and for the safety of the flying public.

Article #10. Remove Preemption

Remove the federal "preemption" which gives airlines immunity from consumer protection laws. Airline passengers have an inalienable right to retain their human rights, one of which is their right to speak when something is wrong on a flight, and another is their right to sue an airline. Our human rights must not be restricted by immunity for the airlines that releases them from their basic obligation to keep people safe.

Reclaiming Our Rights

Perhaps you now realize, dear reader, that passengers will have to join in the fight to regain their rights, similar to the way nonsmokers had to fight for their right to smoke-free air.

Achieving smoke-free flights was a hard fight that I participated in for many years. When the airlines finally agreed to smoke-free flights, they dragged it on 12 more years, instituting it incrementally beginning with flights under 2 hours.

Smoke-free air travel, as we know it today on all U.S. airliners, represents years of hard work by consumer activists. Passengers and crew can be grateful to the many people involved every time they take a breath of air on an airliner.

The history of no-smoking air travel is an excellent example of a successful consumer activist movement and a great model for changing other unhealthy and hazardous airline policies.

We now need to join together to ban substances such as pesticides that dangerously contaminate the air on airplanes.

We need to keep in mind that enforcement is key in any future aviation regulations. It can no longer be left to the airlines to regulate themselves or to each passenger to battle case by case with the airlines.

Dear readers, you are cordially invited to join me in airline passenger activism.

—Arthur Speigelman, Reuters (New York)

"The self-help book has reached new heights thanks to a grounded former airline stewardess who single-handedly has written, published and promoted the first book on how to survive the discomforts of flying. Her labor of love is a privately-printed paper back called **Jet Smart**. Want to know why you can barely breathe on some flights? Want to know how to sleep on a jet or whether to eat the insipid airline food or bring your own? Want a few coping strategies for jetlag? It's all in **Jet Smart**. Fairechild says she worked on the book for 14 years. And she also acted as a private detective quite a few times, thinking up reasons to sneak into the cockpit to see if the pilots had reduced the airflow for passengers while maintaining it for themselves. She could check the airflow by glancing at the position of a series of toggles on the control panel. Reducing the airflow for passengers by a third is part of what Fairechild calls 'the budget monster'—a cost saving move by the airlines to save $80 an hour in fuel costs. The result is to leave some passengers gasping for breath..."

The Fair Air Coalition

TO THE READER:
> You can make a difference.

From: Sara Held, sara@flyana.com
       FAC Volunteer Coordinator

The Fair Air Coalition is a tax-exempt, non-profit, advocacy organization for the benefit of airline passengers. The Coalition is involved in:

- Focusing media attention on aviation safety and health issues.
- Educating legislators and the flying public on flight-induced maladies.
- Researching and documenting health problems related to flying.
- Providing testimony linking airline passenger health problems to aircraft toxicity.

Through a full-time schedule of research, writing, and media interviews, Diana Fairechild has created The Fair Air Coalition and has been its primary funder.

Her single-handed efforts have enlightened passengers about the health hazards of flying. Both crew and passengers are now aware of the toxic air and water, dangerous pesticides and radiation, and much more on airplanes.

Diana's efforts have directly contributed to government policy changes, so that hundreds of thousands of passengers each year are now, at least, spared pesticide showers in certain cities.

This is only the tip of the iceberg. You can see by "Fairechild's Passenger Bill of Rights" that much more needs to be done.

Diana Fairechild has subsidized almost the entire effort of The Fair Air Coalition through her writing, lobbying, and media interviews. As her work has become more well known and The Fair Air Coalition is now more successful, volunteers' help and contributions are needed in many areas:

• **Administrative Assistance**. The FAC needs help with the voluminous correspondence Diana's activism generates.

• **Web Development**. To increase passenger participation in documenting air travel hazards, The Fair Air Coalition seeks to provide Email access to online passenger questionnaires, and many networking opportunities.

• **Funding**. Funds are needed for essential items, such as air quality testing equipment to monitor in-flight cabin air.

We suggest you carefully document your flights, especially if you have complaints. Then send complaints to your airline's CEO, as well as to the Aviation Subcommittees in both houses of Congress (Senate and House), and also to the head of the FAA (Administrator). Please be sure to send a copy to The Fair Air Coalition.

Yes, you can make a difference. Your efforts and your donations are urgently needed.

Expert Witness

Prior Expert Testimony

• Wrongful death on international flight. Diana Fairechild provided expert witness testimony, Northern California District Court, Rubina Husain vs. Olympic Airways (C99-1400 CRB).

The Decision on 8/28/00 included a finding of willful misconduct on the part of the airline.

From plaintiffs' attorney: "Judge Breyer specifically quoted you to support his finding that Olympic had committed willful misconduct and therefore could not benefit from the liability limits. Your testimony was very effective."

• Passenger injury going down a slide. Diana Fairechild prepared testimony, California Superior Court, Sehgal and Mithal vs. United Airlines (No. 303309).

The case settled on 2/6/01.

From plaintiffs' attorney: "Your experience and research were perfect. You equipped me with nine or ten points that were like fire crackers, giving me the specifics and confidence I needed to push for and achieve a positive settlement for my clients."

National Law Journal
> "Fairechild decisively deals with thorny and in many cases previously undisclosed in-flight environmental issues."

About flyana.com

Diana Fairechild is the creator, webmaster, and writer of flyana.com.

"Flyana" was Diana's nickname when she was a flight attendant, flying 10 million miles around the world for 21 years.

Flyana.com offers over 60 pages of free and up-to-date information for airline passengers including "Fast Facts" for last-minute reminders.

Surveys are occasionally conducted, and comments from readers are regularly posted.

The site's focus is to help readers fly more safely, efficiently, and healthfully.

Diana has great plans for flyana.com. Please check back as the spirit moves you.

The New York Times
    "One of twelve most creative Web sites."

NBC-LA Award
    "The Best of the Web 2000."

International Association of Protection Specialists
    "THE best air travel survival resource."

Los Angeles Times
    "A well-researched, engagingly personal series of columns."

Books by Fairechild

Office Yoga
At-Your-Desk Exercises

Fairechild has practiced yoga since she was a college student in Paris in the 60s. She refined her yoga practice during 50 trips to India—made when she was an international flight attendant.

Now, at the computer for long periods, she felt a need to share her yoga skills with others.

This book has sections for reducing pain and eyestrain, and increasing productivity. Working for long hours at a computer can cause back pain, headaches, and even mood swings, if you are not aware and take care.

With **Office Yoga**, all it takes is 5 seconds to 3 minutes, and you don't even need to leave your desk. These exercises are easy and fun.

Carol McCullough-Dieter, Oracle 8 For Dummies
> "**Office Yoga** should be required
> reading for anyone who works at a
> computer. Wow! Instant energy."

Sue Shellenbarger, The Wall Street Journal
> "I give office yoga an A."

Wil Welsh, Kauai Magazine
> "Clearly written and thoroughly
> illustrated, **Office Yoga** is a treasure
> for anyone who works as a desk."

Noni
Aspirin of the Ancients

In these times when our immune systems are compromised by the air we breathe and the food we eat, it is reassuring to know that there is at least one food which can reverse the effects of toxins—and that is noni.

Fairechild was introduced to noni by native Hawaiians who suggested it as an antidote to the pain and physical disabilities she suffered as a result of two decades spent working in airplanes.

According to Fairechild, noni works on the body the way a good mechanic works on your car. It primes and balances your body to the point that the problem—no matter what it is—no longer exists.

Jonathan Kirsch, book reviewer, Los Angeles
"Fairechild is an authentic visionary and a gifted writer. Her latest book is a wonderful example of the healing spirit she brings to all her work."

Dee Dowdy, reader, San Francisco
"I just finished Noni. Loved it! Was moved to tears. I am enrolled in having a personal relationship with noni, too. Thanks for your great contribution with this book."

Air Travel Books

2003-2004, The Jet Safe & Easy Series
Making the Skies Friendly Again

What happened to the friendly skies? It used to be that the passenger was always right. Today, it's risky even to argue with a flight attendant.

Business people used to imagine flying as a way to meet important contacts, and stewardesses envisioned meeting their husbands. Today, you worry about meeting your Maker at the hands of a suicide terrorist.

So what is flying today? Contaminated air, water, and blankets; inedible airline meals; air rage; radiation; sardine seating; deep vein thrombosis; toxins; delays; lost luggage—and then there are the terrorists.

In keeping with the new consciousness in the country, it's better to be prepared than be afraid. How *do* you prepare for the hazards, hardships, and hassles of flying?

Aviation safety expert, Diana Fairechild, thoroughly addresses all our post 9-11 air travel concerns in **The Jet Safe & Easy Series.**

Based on her voluminous correspondence with readers over the last 11 years, the Series is comprised of 70 chapters in 10 volumes.

Check for release dates of the volumes on flyana.com. Chapters will also be available online to download for a modest fee.

2003, Volume 1. Strategies for the Wise Passenger: Turbulence, Terrorism, Streaking, Cardiac Arrest, Too Tall

1999, 2003, Jet Smarter
The Air Traveler's Rx

This update of **Jet Smart** has been widely quoted by the media as a resource on how to cope with the upsets and indignities of flying.

General Electric Corporate Newsletter
> "Required reading for anyone interested in better, smarter air travel—the perfect gift for anyone who flies and a useful tool for business travelers."

Arlene Ash, reader, Atlanta
> "**Jet Smarter** can save your health, maybe even your life! The book is full of solutions, in depth, comprehensive, and entertaining. Diana's suggestions really work. It's obvious that she's been there, done that, and fixed that herself."

1992, 1994, Jet Smart
200 Tips For Beating Jetlag

The worldwide best seller that pushed Washington to change its policies and has helped millions to survive travel in comfort and style.

Forbes magazine
> "Prepare to be shocked."

About the Author

~~ ~~ ~~
~~ ~~ ~~

My airline career began in 1966 as a Pan American World Airways international stewardess. I was single, healthy, bilingual, and taking birth-control pills.

Worldwide, as we Pan Am stews pranced through airports in our high heels, tight skirts and girdles, white gloves, pill box hats, identical hair cuts, and pretty youthful faces, we looked like a multi-racial dance troop or a flock of exotic birds.

I was hired by Pan Am when air travel was still relatively exclusive and not without risks. Here's an example of what it was like to fly around the world during the glory days of Pan Am. One night, flying somewhere over Asia, a British, first-class passenger told me that wherever wars broke out, it was always more important for him to know the local Pan Am station manager than to know his country's ambassador—it was the station manager who could get him on a plane out of the war zone.

Here's another example. One day on the crew bus leaving Hong Kong, the first officer told us that the night before he had missed the last ferry from Hong Kong to Kowloon (where our hotel was), so he had to hire a private boat. The boatman evidently assumed that our out-of-uniform pilot was a foreigner with the usual appetites and asked him, "You want nice girl?"

"No, thank you," the pilot said. A few minutes later, the boatman asked the same question. This time, our pilot, wanting to stop this conversation, replied, "I only like American girls."

"*Ay-ya*," said the boatman. "The only *bakgui* [white ghost] lady in Hong Kong is Pan Am stew."

In 1966, Pan Am bragged that among its 4,000 stews, 38 languages were spoken. We stews had a glamorous life and picked our flights each month from among 94 cities on 6 continents.

Also in 1966, Pan Am surprised the world when it announced its plans to be the first airline to buy jets that could carry over 400 passengers.

Of course, this was the Boeing 747. Pan Am eventually purchased 40 Boeing 747s—and I eventually flew just about all of them as chief purser to every corner of the globe.

Going With The Flow

Pan Am went bankrupt in the 80s, and our 60s hand-tailored uniform has long been retired, but you can still get a flavor of the times by watching the 2002 film, "Catch Me If You Can." It shows a bevy of Pan Am stews in the 60s turning all heads and hearts at Miami Airport.

Flying was certainly fun, but while flitting around the world, my own health problems took me in an unexpected direction. I had to focus on my health, or I couldn't handle all the night flying and time zone changes. The jetlag was horrific, and I had to stay on my toes or I became ill.

While serving my passengers, I observed that flying affected their health as well, and I became concerned for them—especially the elderly, the occasional child, and frequent flyers, who like us never seemed to catch up on their jetlag.

On board, while offering hot towels, drinks, food, and landing forms, healthy flying ideas began to flow into my mind—and I wrote them down on Pan Am cocktail napkins and food order forms.

At home I typed and retyped my notes. As soon as personal computers came out, I got one. I wrote in all my spare time—there was a momentum inside me. The writing energized me and had a life of its own. This book you now hold in your hands is a direct result of my own health problems, which were caused by flying.

Near-Fatal Blood Clot

My second year with Pan Am I nearly died from a blood clot that started with an injury on the plane. While boarding, the aluminum door at the top of the runway stairs to the plane blew shut and hit my leg. My hands were full with heavy bags, so I couldn't stop the door from slamming on my leg.

In those days, chief pursers carried all the first class silver serving utensils, including the roast beef carving knife. Imagine tweezers being taken away from flight attendants today, when I used to fly with a 9-inch serrated knife in my bag.

After takeoff, I was busy—and it wasn't until 12 hours later when we arrived in Tokyo that I noticed my leg was swollen. I didn't see a doctor and worked my next flight home, and a few days later I woke up with a sharp pain in my lung. It was almost impossible to take a breath. In the hospital, I was told that I had nearly died when a blood clot that had formed in my injured leg (deep vein thrombosis) passed through my heart. And that this clot was now in my lung (pulmonary embolism).

After 6 months, I went back to flying and all seemed well. Only 30 years later did I understand that the blood clot was flight-related. There are certain conditions on the plane which make it easier for blood clots to form. These aircraft environmental factors start with the onboard low air pressure and low humidity.

On top of this, or should I say *under* this, my "required" uniform girdle contributed to the propensity of my blood to clot after the injury. The girdle cut off circulation at high altitude when the body automatically swells up.

Then there were the birth control pills that changed my body chemistry, so I was in an "at-risk" category.

Flying, birth control pills, and a leg injury can be a dangerous combination.

Looking back, I see that no matter how painful and shocking, this blood clot was a blessing in disguise. Life became more precious after this incident, and I felt compelled to do something useful with mine.

After nearly dying in my early 20s, I focused on helping others. My venue was air travel and passenger advocacy, which became my life's work.

119

I Learn About Fresh Air

As a result of the pulmonary embolism, I became very sensitive to toxins in the air. I remember well one flight after deregulation when my left lung was hurting and I discovered that the pilot had deliberately reduced the fresh air supply in the cabin (for the passengers and flight attendants).

Subsequently, I learned that pilots routinely reduced the fresh air for passengers—but not for themselves—in order to save fuel.

As time went by, I noticed that when the fresh air was reduced, I had trouble thinking. For example, as chief purser, I had to tally the accounts (from liquor, headsets, and duty-free purchases) at the end of every flight.

When there was plenty of fresh air, I had no problem doing the accounts, which included currency conversions.

But when the air was recirculated, I found I always had trouble with the accounting, as well as difficulty breathing, and pain in my lung.

Deregulation Nearly Kills Me

During my first 12 years of flying, I felt safe on planes in spite of the blood clot incident. At work, I felt energized and tremendously enjoyed my passengers.

The passenger-to-stewardess ratio in those days, by the way, was double what it is today.

By far, the worst change that came about after deregulation was the recirculated air—we now got less than 50 percent fresh air. On top of that, passengers were jammed in closer together, so more people were competing for the meager fresh air that trickled in through the air vents.

Deregulation achieved its goals of increased competition and lower airfares—the number of airlines doubled, the number of passengers doubled, and airfares went down. But now, looking back from where the airlines are today, deregulation came at a terrible price in unacknowledged health consequences for passengers and crew. For my part, the working conditions became so poor that this resulted in the complete collapse of my health.

Pesticides In Planes

Today, many areas of airline travel concern me. The most disturbing is the use of pesticides in occupied cabins.

On certain international routes, poison is actually sprayed right on passengers. During the years that I flew, I was in airplanes when they were sprayed with pesticide hundreds of times.

The poison got in my lungs, on my skin, and in my eyes. Over the years, my body became more vulnerable to these poisons.

Medical Grounding

The weakness that descended on me was insidious—I kept thinking I would get over it, but it only got worse.

During my last year of flying, 1987, I fell ill on every flight and had to use my days off to recover with the aid of medicine and bed rest. I spent all my time off in bed trying to recuperate for my next flight.

Finally, I was "medically grounded" with flu-like symptoms that persisted for years. As it turned out, I spent the next decade and a half struggling with my health.

On top of this, not being able to fly was a great personal loss. Flying had been much more than a job—for 21 years I had had an enchanting lifestyle traveling around the globe.

122

    I was diagnosed with "chemical poisoning" by George Ewing, M.D., Chief of Allergy at Straub Hospital in Honolulu.

    Three other specialists in environmental medicine subsequently confirmed this diagnosis. They all said the cause of the poisoning was toxins in the planes where I worked.

    It was a shock to find out that my health problems were caused by conditions on the plane.

    I felt as if I had been driving along obeying all the traffic signals, but suddenly my wheels were spinning and I could no longer handle the car.

    I had become so acutely sensitive to toxins that I couldn't function in any so-called "normal" environment—around anyone wearing chemicals, even fabric softener in their clothes or deodorant, and certainly not perfume or lotion. My eyes were acutely sensitive to light, and I was very weak.

Years Of Healing & Reflection

The pain of those years is still so biting it is easier to speak of them metaphorically. . . *I'm on a trapeze.* I've been flying along, doing stunts on the bar. Suddenly, I can't see the catcher. I have to let go of the bar because I can't hold on any more. There is no catcher! I fall.

And then a whole new world opens up to me. I discover a safety net that turns out to be okay, and then, ultimately, a pretty interesting place.

But the safety net is not a permanent place, and I have had to let go again, and again. I'm getting kind of used to it now—letting go. Living on faith. Surrendering to the present challenges.

Situations keep changing, but I keep managing in ways I never could have dreamed of while holding the bar, trying to hold on to my job with the airlines, holding fast even while my health was declining.

124

Birthing Jet Smart

For many years, I hardly left home. I wrote about air travel and eventually published **Jet Smart** in 1992 at a time when I was still too ill to go on a book tour.

After an initial write up in a Hawaiian newspaper, Rotary Clubs around the state began to invite me to speak. Hawaii is a tourist destination, and many Rotarians at these meetings are tourists.

I thank all these Rotarians—they used to line up after my talks to buy autographed copies of **Jet Smart**. Then they took my books all over the world and talked about my work.

Barely 13 months after **Jet Smart** came out, a *USA Today* feature called it "An underground hit," and Xerox, Johnson & Johnson, and General Motors had purchased **Jet Smart** in bulk—GM bought them for a convention in Detroit.

Jet Smart Readers Bring Change

I was quoted by many newspapers and magazines (*New York Times, Forbes, Business Week, International Herald Tribune, London Times, Taipei Times, Tokyo Today, Veja Brazil*), and interviewed on syndicated radio shows such as Art Bell—all from home.

Dateline, ABC News, and Hard Copy flew to Hawaii to interview me. CNN TV had me on air answering questions for an hour.

There were hundreds of interviews in a couple of years because **Jet Smart** broke dozens of stories about airline health and safety practices and policies. Here are a few well-known examples:

• **Jet Smart** broke the story about contaminated drinking water on planes and the lack of potable drinking water for passengers. My allegations were proven 7 years later by a Japanese study, and then again in 2002 by a *Wall Street Journal* report.

• **Jet Smart** first broke the story about the dangerously high levels of toxins on board. A toxin is a substance that can cause death, mutations, reproductive malfunctions, diseases, and behavioral problems in people, in animals, and in their offspring. Subsequently, there have been lawsuits against airlines based on chemical toxicity.

• **Jet Smart** broke the story that pilots get to breathe better air and that they deliberately reduce the oxygen in the passenger cabins to save money for the airlines.

Whenever I was in the cockpit, I could tell that the air was fresher and richer. And once I learned where the fresh air toggle switches were located on the cockpit instrument panel, I used to verify my perceptions with the switches—though I could always tell anyway because of the pain in my lung. But pilots vigorously denied that they had better quality air.

Even years later, after both *USA Today* and *Smart Money* quoted me about cockpit vs. cabin air, a few pilots wrote to these publications, pecking at my credibility.

The airlines finally admitted the truth in a press release about smoke-free flights, saying passengers were guaranteed smoke-free air even if a pilot smoked because the cockpit had separate air.

• **Jet Smart** first broke the story about the horrific practice of spraying pesticides on airline passengers while trying to kill agricultural insects.

A worldwide investigation followed, and at least 20 countries stopped spraying pesticides in occupied aircraft cabins.

But dozens of countries still require the airlines to spray while passengers are on board. Ongoing advocacy is urgently needed.

You may wonder why I toot my own horn about being the first to bring these and other safety issues to the public.

First, I feel that it is important to occasionally attend to my professional record in order to maintain the highest degree of effectiveness and credibility in advancing my cause.

And I'd also like you to know, dear readers, that there is at least one recognized expert who will continue to speak the truth, regardless of pressures from the airline industry. ⅅ